My Little Lore of Light

A Child's Version of
Lore of Light

by
Hajjah Amina Adil

Retold and Illustrated By
Karima Sperling

Naqshbandi-Haqqani Sufi Order of America

© 2005 Naqshbandi-Haqqani Sufi Order of America

All rights reserved. No part of this book may be reproduced, stored in a retrieval system, or transmitted in any form, or by any means, electronic, mechanical, photocopying, or otherwise, without the written permission of the Naqshbandi-Haqqani Sufi Order.

ISBN: 1-930409-67-5

Library of Congress Cataloging-in-Publication Data

Adil, Hajjah Amina.
  My little Lore of light : a child's version of Lore of light / by Hajja Amina Adil ; retold and illustrated By Karima Sperling.
     p. cm.
   ISBN 1-930409-35-4
   1. Prophets, Pre-Islamic--Juvenile literature. 2. Legends, Islamic--Juvenile literature. I. Title: Lore of light. II. Sperling, Karima. III. Title.
   BP137.A35 2005
   297.2'46--dc22
                              2005009437

Published and Distributed by:
Naqshbandi-Haqqani Sufi Order of America
17195 Silver Parkway, #201
Fenton, MI 48430 USA
Tel: (888) 278-6624
Fax: (810) 815-0518
Email: staff@naqshbandi.org

Original Library of Congress Control Number:
ISBN: 1-930409-35-4

On the Internet, please visit
www.naqshbandi.org
for more titles in Islamic spirituality and traditional scholarship.

Note on the Illustrations

Representation of the prophets has been problematical among certain groups within Islam. However, many great Islamic civilizations illustrated their histories and stories of the prophets. This present work was designed to inspire and inform young modern Muslim children and aid them in remembering their prophets. The pictures were deemed functional and necessary to accomplish this aim. The style of drawing was adapted from an early classical Islamic text, the *Jami' al Tavarikh,* by Rashid al Din. The pictures were kept flat and two-dimensional and are intended as mnemonic devices symbolizing ideas or themes rather than as realistic portrayals.

Note to the Children

You will notice that the faces are left empty. There is a reason for this. The light of Muhammad ﷺ shone so brightly on the faces of Allah's Prophets that their beauty was unlike that of other people. When the people looked at the faces of their Prophets they saw light and love and everything that was most beautiful. We cannot picture this light or love on paper. We cannot draw faces that to everyone will look the most beautiful. So we leave the faces without features and let our imaginations picture them in our minds. In this way we will show our respect for the finest of Allah's creation and keep the light and the love for His prophets safe in our hearts.

Also you will notice that each time a prophet or an angel is mentioned there is some Arabic that follows such as ﷷ. This phrase is pronounced, *'alaihi salaam,* and means, "On him be peace." In the Qur'an Allah speaks of sending peace on His prophets and so we ask that He continue to do this when we remember all they have done for us. Following the mention of the most beloved Prophet Muhammad ﷺ you will find a different Arabic phrase, *salla llahu 'alaihi was sallim,* which means, "Allah bless him and give him peace." This special blessing, reserved only for the Prophet ﷺ himself, is the blessing that Qur'an says that Allah and His angels are sending on Muhammad ﷺ. Next to the names of companions of the prophets and saints you will find the phrase, ﷸ/ﷺ, *radia llahu 'an,* which means, "Allah be pleased with him or her." Allah asked us in the Qur'an to show love and respect for His special servants, His friends, and so we honor even the mention of their names. It is a good thing to learn to do.

Dedication

We begin in the Name of Allah the Most Merciful, the Most Compassionate, and pray that He find some good in our efforts and that He bless them with usefulness in the fulfillment of His Will.

This work is dedicated to Hajjah Amina Adil whose four volumes of *Lore of Light* served as inspiration and source for this small book. Her stories give life to the past and meaning to the present. Until her passing in 2004, Hajjah Amina continued a time-honored tradition in using the stories of the Prophets to teach and enthrall the circle of women and children who gathered around her. As soon as they are able, children should be encouraged to read her original books. Many difficult choices had to be made regarding the material to be included in this abridged account. I beg her pardon and that of the reader for any errors or poor choices in the present work.

This book is also dedicated to her daughter, Hajjah Naziha Kabbani, whose idea it was to make a book for young children from her mother's work. I thank her from my heart for her inspiration and wisdom and her beautiful example of grace and humor in all circumstances.

Of course, as with all our efforts, this book is done for the love and honor of our Prophet Muhammad Mustapha ﷺ and his representative, our master, Shaykh Nazim al Haqqani, and his Khalif, Shaykh Muhammad

Hisham Kabbani. The light of Muhammad ﷺ shines so brightly from their faces that (God willing) even I can follow it. May Allah bless them all and forgive me.

Acknowledgements

Thanks go always to Allah, Lord of the worlds, for continuing in His Mercy to send us guidance. All Light is His and to Him is our journey.

Thank you to Radhia Shukrullah without whose beautiful translation we would never have had Hajjah Amina's words in English.

Thank you to my family whose patience and help were far-reaching, especially to Aminah, who did so much of the typing and all the computer work, to Alia who helped with the drawings for the cover, and to Munir who edited.

Thank you to Hamza El-Din, Mahmoud and Aliya Shelton and family for their support and in depth proof reading of the text.

Thank you to Tara Dalton for her expert artistic advice and computer skills.

Thank you to Taher Siddiqui for all his help and patience.
Thank you to Aminah Sperling for the color edition, and new cover.

Table of Contents

Note on the Illustrations iv

Note to the Children v

Dedication vi

Acknowledgements viii

In the Beginning. 2

1 And the Light Passed to Adam ﷺ 6

2 And the Light Passed to Seth ﷺ 12

3 And the Light Passed to Idris ﷺ 16

4 The Light Passed to Nuh ﷺ 22

5 The Light Passed to Hood ﷺ 28

6 And the Light Passed to Salih ﷺ 34

7 And the Light Passed to Ibrahim ﷺ 40

8 And the Light Passed to Ismail ﷺ 46

9 And the Light Passed to Lut ﷺ 52

10 And the Light Passed to Ishaq ﷺ 58

11 And the Light Passed to Ya'qub ﷺ 64

12 And the Light Passed to Yusuf ﷺ 70

13 And the Light Passed to Ayyoub ﷺ 76

14 And the Light Passed to Dhul-Kifl ﷺ 82

15 And the Light Passed to Shu'ayb ﷺ 88

16 And the light passed to Musa ﷺ 92

17 And the Light Passed also to Harun ﷺ 98

18 And the Light Passed to Yusha ﷺ 104

19 And the Light Passed to Samuel ﷺ 110

20 And the Light Passed to Da'ud ﷺ 116

21 And the Light Passed to Luqman ﷺ 120

22 And the Light Passed to Sulayman ﷺ..124

23 And the Light Passed to Iliyas ﷺ...130

24 And the Light Passed to Alyas'a ﷺ...136

25 And the Light Passed to Yunus ﷺ..142

26 And the Light Passed to Sha'ya ﷺ...148

27 And the Light Passed to Armiya ﷺ..152

28 And the Light Passed to Daniel ﷺ...156

29 And the Light Passed to Uzair ﷺ..160

30 And the Light Passed to Dhul-Qarnain ﷺ....................................164

31 And the Light Passed to Zakaria ﷺ...170

32 And the Light Passed to Yahya ﷺ...174

33 And the Light Passed to 'Isa ﷺ..178

34 And the Light Returned to Muhammad ﷺ...................................184

And those who believe in Allah and His Messengers and make no distinction between any of them, to them He will grant their rewards. (4:152)

In the Beginning

Before Allah created any other thing He created from His own Light the light of the Prophet Muhammad ﷺ. No other thing existed at the time, not heaven or hell, not stars or earth, not sun or moon, not angel or man. Only this light existed.

Then Allah willed the whole creation to "Be," and in six days He created all of the world as we know it and many things we do not know. Into each of these creations He placed a portion of this light of Muhammad ﷺ. The sky got a portion. The angels got a portion. The earth, the trees, the animals, the plants, the stones, all got their portion of the light.

The light that remained Allah placed in a lamp of green emerald that He hung from the tree called "Certainty" in the Garden of Paradise.

Then He stopped to listen. The whole world vibrated with love of the God Who had made it. And Allah knew that He needed a guardian to watch over that precious world and its many creatures.

Allah ordered the Angel Azrail ؑ to bring to Him dirt from the surface of the earth. The angel obeyed and gathered a bit of dirt from each of the corners of the earth. Azrail ؑ brought red dirt and brown dirt, black dirt and white dirt, yellow dirt and orange dirt, and placed them all before his Creator, Allah Almighty. Allah added to the dirt of many colors some water from the springs of Paradise and the dirt became clay. From this clay He fashioned the beautiful form of the Prophet Adam ﷺ.

Allah breathed into this lifeless form and it became soft and alive. Then He placed on Adam's ﷺ forehead a portion of the light of Muhammad ﷺ, and gave Adam ﷺ the gift of knowledge of the names of all creation.

Adam ﷺ looked and saw this light streaming in front of him like a headlight and he asked his Creator about it. Allah told him that it was given to him in trust. Adam ﷺ must take care of it and honor it, and this light would pass from him to his children and from them to their children. But each of them must guard this precious light, keeping it pure and keeping it bright by keeping pure and bright themselves in harmony with Allah's Will. From pure parent to pure child, from kind parent to kind child, from upright parent to upright child, the light would pass, generation after generation until it would reach its destination on the forehead of the pure soul of the Prophet Muhammad ﷺ.

All of us carry some of this light, inherited from our great grandfather Adam ﷺ deep inside us. But only from the Prophets and their friends, the saints, does it shine on the forehead like a beacon and illuminate all the darkness around them.

And because without light there would only be dense darkness we must always search for this light before and behind us, within and without us and guard it and honor it until the end of days.

This then is the story of that light.

So come along as we follow the light of Muhammad ﷺ on its journey through the ages, from heart to heart, from forehead to forehead, from the creation of the Prophet Adam ﷺ to the birth of the last Prophet, Muhammad Mustafa ﷺ.

Adam ﷺ

I (Allah) will make for the earth someone to rule in My Name. (2:30)

I

And the Light Passed to Adam ﷺ

After the creation of Adam ﷺ, Allah stood him before the angels and his beauty amazed them. Then Allah commanded Adam ﷺ to tell the angels their names and the names of all the wonderful creation. And his wisdom amazed them. Allah commanded the inhabitants of heaven to bow down before Adam ﷺ. They bowed down low before the light of Muhammad ﷺ streaming from Adam's ﷺ brow.

All bowed except one whose name was Iblis. He refused to bow to a creature of dirt while he was made of fire. He was jealous of Adam ﷺ. He disobeyed his Creator and for this he was sent away from the heavenly company. In anger he vowed to destroy Adam ﷺ and his children, to forever haunt them and tempt them and lead them into disobedience. He would prove to his Lord that he had been right not to bow to a thing of dirt. Allah allowed him to test Adam ﷺ. This was all part of His plan, because light can only be truly appreciated when it comes after and changes the darkness. Iblis is the darkness, which we call Shaytan or the Devil.

Allah put Adam ﷺ to live in the heavenly Garden of Paradise, and he lived there worshipping Allah in peace and happiness for a long time. Then

Adam ﷺ became lonely and he asked Allah for a companion. While Adam ﷺ slept Allah took a rib from Adam's ﷺ chest and from it fashioned a beautiful woman. When Adam ﷺ awoke he knew her immediately because Allah had already taught him the names of all things. Adam ﷺ knew her to be Hawwa ؑ, his wife. They married in the garden and began to live together in joy. Allah gave them the whole garden except for the wheat tree which He told them to leave alone, never to touch.

Iblis saw his chance. He stood by the gate of Paradise crying until the peacock came and asked the reason. Iblis told him about death that must come to every living thing. The only cure, Iblis told the peacock, was to eat the fruit of the forbidden tree of wheat. The peacock told the snake. The snake told Hawwa ؑ and Hawwa ؑ, fearful of death, ate from the tree and convinced Adam ﷺ also to eat from it.

They had done the one thing that they were forbidden. Out of fear they had disobeyed Allah and they were terribly sorry. They asked to be forgiven but the time was not right and Allah sent them from Paradise as He had Iblis. From then on they could live only on the earth. Adam ﷺ descended on a mountain in Sri Lanka and Hawwa ؑ descended in a desert in Arabia. They were desperately lonely and full of sorrow. They cried for forgiveness and searched for each other.

Now this was all in accordance with Allah's Will. He had made Adam ﷺ to be guardian over the earth, a thing he could not do while living in Paradise. But in His ultimate Mercy Allah gave this sorrow to Adam ﷺ and Hawwa ؑ and all their children after them. Deep inside all of us is an emptiness, an unnamed longing for the peace and safety of Paradise. Allah's parting gift to man was an aching homesickness that would protect him against the temptations of Shaytan and prevent him from ever being completely at home anywhere except close to Allah in Paradise.

After many ages of crying and asking for forgiveness, Adam ﷺ and Hawwa ﷺ were finally forgiven, and Adam ﷺ came to join Hawwa ﷺ in Arabia.

They began to have children. All their first children were born as fraternal twins, a boy and a girl, and they were ordered to marry each other's twin and start families of their own, because, of course, there were no others.

But one of the boys, Qabil, was jealous of his brother, Habil ﷺ. Inspired by the jealous Iblis he wanted his brother's wife and most of all he wanted the light that shone from his brother's brow. He determined to get rid of Habil ﷺ. Qabil hit Habil ﷺ with a rock and stood back in horror. There had been no death before this and no violence. Qabil felt great regret about what he had done. He lifted the lifeless body of his brother and carried it in his arms from place to place for a long time having no idea what he should do with it. Finally the crow, in pity, taught him to scratch the earth and bury Habil ﷺ inside, but nowhere could he bury the grief he felt. He left his parents and took his family to wander the world looking for peace, in all the wrong places.

Adam ﷺ and Hawwa ﷺ were full of sorrow at the loss of two of their sons, but most of all, they sorrowed at the loss of the light of Muhammad ﷺ and they prayed to Allah to grant them another good son to carry that light.

They had many, many children, all of them twins except one son, who was born single. He was the one chosen by Allah to replace the murdered Habil ﷺ, good and obedient enough to carry that precious light into the future.

May Allah bless Adam ﷺ and give him peace.

Seth ﷺ

Oh children of Adam did I not make a covenant with you? (36:60)

2

And the Light Passed to Seth ﷺ

The child who inherited the light of Muhammad ﷺ from his father Adam ﷺ was Seth ﷺ. His name means "Gift of God," and he was holy and a Prophet. Seth ﷺ was very beautiful, resembling his murdered brother Habil ﷺ in almost every way. Adam ﷺ and Hawwa ﷺ rejoiced to see the light shine from his forehead, like the beacon on a lighthouse.

Adam ﷺ took a promise from Seth ﷺ that he would marry a good woman and lead his life according to Allah's Way and raise his children to be upright after him. The promise was witnessed by a host of angels who descended with a gift from their Lord. Allah sent to Seth ﷺ a treasure chest in which was stored his promise and the descriptions of all the great Prophets and Messengers that would follow among his descendants so that they could be known and recognized by the wise among the people. This chest later came to be called the "Ark (chest) of the Covenant (promise)," and it was a very sacred and precious thing. It would be passed on from Prophet to Prophet along with the light. As long as it was in their hands the believing people would be safe.

In the beginning men lived a very long time. When he was 400 years old

Seth ﷺ buried his father Adam ﷺ who had lived to the ripe old age of 1,000 years. Seth ﷺ fathered many children and lived with them in the mountains near Damascus. He and his children were farmers and shepherds. They lived peaceably on the land. Some of the other children of Adam ﷺ however, were not so obedient, and they lived in the valleys near the waterways and were lazy and made trouble for others.

Seth ﷺ died at 720 years, after fulfilling his promise and passing the light and the Ark to his son Enush ﷺ.

Enush ﷺ passed the light to Kan'aan ﷺ, and Kan'aan ﷺ to Mahalalel ﷺ, and Mahalalel ﷺ to Yerad ﷺ.

May Allah bless Seth ﷺ and give him peace.

Idris ﷺ

He was a man of truth, a Prophet, and We raised him to an elevated place.

(19:56-57)

3

And the Light Passed to Idris ﷺ

Yerad ﷺ was worried when the angels announced the birth of his son. Would he be able to raise him to keep the light pure and the promise unbroken? There were so many young people losing their way, doing things that were forbidden and forgetting their Lord. Was it possible, he worried, to raise a pure child among all the evil in the world? To his immense relief when his baby son was born he saw the light of Muhammad ﷺ shining from his forehead like the sun.

Yerad ﷺ named his son Idris ﷺ, the learned one, and he became a great prophet and messenger to his people. He taught them, by Allah's will, so many of the things that we now take for granted. It would be hard to imagine a world without the knowledges that Idris ﷺ brought.

He learned to kindle fire by which to keep warm and cook.

He learned, from the spider, to spin yarn from the wool of the sheep that he herded and to weave it into cloth. He then cut it between two sharp rocks to make clothes. Idris ﷺ became a tailor for his people.

He learned to write down the word of Allah and to read it back, and then to bind it together in a book. Idris ﷺ became a teacher to his people.

He learned to count and to keep track of the numbers by adding and subtracting. He studied the stars and learned their movements and how to navigate by them. He became the first astronomer and a guide to his people.

He studied the plants and learned which ones were good for healing. He became a doctor to his people.

But most of all he taught God's laws, the Religion of Adam ﷺ, and he was a Prophet to his people.

After 250 years the unbelieving people living in the valleys became jealous and they assembled an army to invade and take all the wonderful things the people of Idris ﷺ had made. To protect his people Idris ﷺ invented the bow and arrow from watching the branch of an apple tree bend and send its fruit flying. He saw metal melt from the stones in a cooking fire. He collected it and made swords and spears. He armed his people.

But the good people who followed Idris ﷺ did not want to hurt even their enemies. Idris ﷺ had to teach them that defending good against evil, right against wrong, is a necessary hardship required by Allah. They should not try to hurt others but they must defend themselves, or there would be no one left on earth to worship the Lord.

They won the first battle. But then the evil men learned to use bows also and to forge swords and spears. Idris ﷺ had to think of something new to keep his people safe. He tamed the wild camel to be ridden in battle. Then he remembered the stories his father had told him of the wonderful beasts Adam ﷺ had seen on his journey from Sri Lanka to China and then to Arabia. Idris ﷺ taught the horse to be a friend to man.

At the end of his very busy life Idris ﷺ retired from people to spend time alone meditating and worshipping God. His prayers were so beautiful that angels would come from their various stations in the universe to sit and worship with him. Each particle of creation, from the smallest grain of rice to the largest star, has its special angels created to watch over it. The one whose companionship he most enjoyed was the angel of the sun.

After many years praying together in Idris' ﷺ house, the angel of the sun received Allah's permission to take Idris ﷺ to visit the place where he resided. They spent many days together in this place of light until the Angel of Death ﷺ slipped in and took Idris' ﷺ soul. The angel of the sun felt badly that his friend should die while he was still his guest and begged Allah to restore Idris' ﷺ soul until he could be returned to earth. Idris ﷺ was made to live again and asked his angelic friend to give him a tour of Paradise before returning him to earth.

But when Idris ﷺ saw the Paradise garden and felt the closeness of his Lord, he determined to stay. There was nothing anyone could do. Idris ﷺ had already died once and Allah had promised us only one death. He was already in Paradise and Allah had promised that whoever enters can never be forced to leave again.

The Prophet Idris ﷺ is of such exalted station that, unlike other men, he entered Paradise alive, where he lives today and some say, is tailor to the angels.

May Allah bless Idris ﷺ and give him peace.

Nuh ﷺ

And it moved on with them amid waves like mountains. (46:24)

4

And the Light Passed to Nuh ﷺ

Idris ﷺ had many children and grandchildren. Among them was a young man named Lamaq. He carried the light of his grandfather Idris ﷺ although he was not a great prophet himself. Lamaq and his wife gave birth to a baby boy and they saw that the light of Muhammad ﷺ shone on his forehead. It streamed out before him like the beacon on a lighthouse that guides ships though the darkness safely to harbor.

They named their son Sakir because he was so sweet, but later he was called Nuh ﷺ because of the difficulties he faced. He was a great prophet.

Nuh ﷺ became a worker in wood. When he was forty years old the Archangel Mikail ﷺ took him on a journey to show him the whole world. Everywhere he looked Nuh ﷺ saw injustice and despair. The wealthy people no longer cared for the poor. The strong no longer protected the weak. Those who had been given great gifts by Allah used these gifts to help only themselves and to hurt others. Nobody remembered their Creator, Allah, or their task to be guardians over His creation. When he returned, Nuh ﷺ began to teach. He traveled in the land and told people about Allah. He told them to treat each other kindly and with fairness. The rich people had him chased away by their guards and the poor people threw stones at him.

For 480 years people made fun of him. And in all that time only 80 men and women listened and followed Nuh ﷺ in worshipping Allah. Nuh ﷺ had a wife and four sons, Sam ﷺ, Ham ﷺ, Japheth ﷺ and Yam. Even his wife and son Yam did not follow him and were among the unbelievers.

Nuh ﷺ was completely disgusted. He prayed to Allah to clean the earth of evil and evildoers. The Lord accepted his prayer. Nuh ﷺ began to sob at the thought of the mighty destruction that his prayer must bring. For this he came to be called Nuh ﷺ, the one who cries out in sorrow.

Allah Almighty commanded Nuh ﷺ to build a great boat. He ordered that this boat be built of 124,000 planks of wood, on each of which should be written the name of one of the Prophets, those that had already come and those yet to come. It should have a prow like the breastbone of a bird and a stern like a peacock's tail. It should be three stories, the bottom for the animals, the middle for the birds and insects, and the top for the people. This boat came to be called the Ark because, like the Ark of Seth ﷺ, it was to be a container of great treasure. In it the good of creation and the names of all the prophets would be saved from destruction.

Nuh ﷺ finished the Ark but nowhere around was there any water; no sea, no lake, not even a pond that could float such a large boat. The bad people now thought that Nuh ﷺ had gone completely crazy and they teased him mercilessly. They began to use his boat for a toilet, until the Ark was covered with filth and smelled so bad that Nuh ﷺ could not go near it. Allah promised Nuh ﷺ that He would make the disbelievers clean the Ark.

The unbelieving people began to get sick. Their bodies were covered with a red and very itchy rash. They were miserable. One day an old man, while going to the toilet on the Ark, slipped and fell into the stinking mess. He found that all his rash had been healed. He told the others and soon they were all rolling around in the filth they had made, even licking it up with their tongues to get every bit of the healing dirt. Before long the Ark was as clean as new.

Now Allah commanded Nuh ﷺ to load up the Ark with food and water and to collect a pair, male and female, of each kind of animal. All the creatures were ordered by Allah to live in peace and kinship with each other for the length of their journey. This boat was a boat of safety and security. Each creature on it wished all the others peace. The lion and the lioness bowed their royal heads when the humble sheep passed by. The tiger and lady tiger spoke in soft voices so as not to startle the nervous gazelle. The bull elephant and his cow lifted their great feet with care and set them down gently among the small animals. Even if the tips of their tails did flick once or twice, the cat and her tom kept their eyes lowered when the mouse and his wife scurried past. On the second floor, the raptor birds, the owls and vultures and eagles, kept their talons clenched around their high perches while the starlings and finches fluttered and played.

Last of all the 80 believers boarded the Ark, and they waited. Soon dark clouds began to gather and it began to pour rain. Water also gushed out of the earth. Wells became pools and streams became rushing rivers. From above and below water gushed. The Ark began to float. Nuh ﷺ called his wife and son but they thought they could outsmart Allah by climbing to the top of the highest mountain. No one can outsmart Allah and even the mountaintops soon disappeared under water. Slowly the people on the Ark watched the dry land disappear with all that was on it. The people, the houses, the trees, all were washed away.

For six months Nuh ﷺ and his followers lived on the Ark, until the water began to go down. Finally on the 10th of Muharram the Ark landed on Mount Judi. The 80 people descended and cooked a last meal from all the food left on the ark, dried fruit and beans, lentils, rice and wheat. They called this concoction Nuh's ﷺ pudding.

They began to build houses and till the soil. Now Allah told Nuh ﷺ to make clay pots from the wet earth left from the flood. Nuh ﷺ made thousands of pots and bowls and after they were dry placed them in a pile as high as a mountain. Then Allah ordered Nuh ﷺ to pull out the bottom pot, making the whole pile fall and shatter into a million pieces. Nuh ﷺ cried in his loss and then cried harder as he realized that Allah had felt a greater loss in the destruction of the whole world, His creation. Nuh ﷺ felt great sorrow and asked Allah to forgive him for praying for that terrible flood.

Nuh ﷺ lived 950 years. His three sons, Sam ﷺ, Ham ﷺ and Japheth ﷺ were the only survivors to have children. All of us are descended from them. The sons of Sam ﷺ settled in Arabia and India, the sons of Japheth ﷺ in Turkey, Persia and Europe, and the sons of Ham ﷺ in Egypt and Africa.

May Allah bless Nuh ﷺ and give him peace.

Hood ﷺ

They said this is a cloud bringing us rain. No it is…a wind in which is painful punishment, destroying everything by the command of its Lord.

(46:24-25)

5

The Light Passed to Hood ﷺ

For 800 years the children of Sam ﷺ lived in the area of Mecca in Arabia. In the beginning the memory of the great flood was fresh in their minds and they kept faithful to their promise and worshipped only The Lord Almighty, their Creator. But little by little, as it happens with the sons of Adam ﷺ, they forgot, until the flood was just a distant legend. The people returned to the worship of false gods.

One group of the children of Sam ﷺ lived in the north of Arabia. They called themselves Ad and they were a large and aggressive people. They took what they wanted from others less strong. They captured the weak and made them slaves while they did no work themselves. They worshipped their King as if he were God and for him they killed innocent victims and served them up for his dinner.

One of the people of Ad was the first to discover gold. He fished it out of the streams and dug it from the rock. He made statues and jewelry and the people began to bow down before it because of its dazzling beauty.

To the royal family of these forgetful people was born a descendant of Nuh ﷺ. They named him Hood ﷺ because unlike the other people of Ad he was kind and mild mannered. Although none of them could see it, from his forehead the light of Muhammad ﷺ shone like the sun breaking through the clouds.

Hood ؊, when he was still quite young, would leave the parties and terrible ceremonies of his people and retreat to a cave in the hills to think and pray. When he was forty years old Allah sent the angel Jibrail ؊ to tell him that he was to be a great Prophet. He must go and teach his people, but he must never, no matter how much his people would demand it, ever show them a miracle because that would lead to their destruction.

Hood ؊ had always felt great sympathy for the slaves of Ad. Not only did they do all the work while their masters slept but they were mistreated and abused. They were fed too little and beaten too much. Hood ؊ took to living with them, and he found among the slaves hearts that were humble and minds that were hungry for Truth. He began to teach them about Allah and the slaves listened and followed their Prophet Hood ؊.

When Hood's ؊ family discovered that he was living with the slaves, sleeping on the ground, eating miserable food, they became worried. They went to him and insisted that he behave as an owner of slaves not as a slave himself. They placed a whip in his hand and demanded that he whip one of the slaves, his friend, or be killed himself. Hood ؊ tried to refuse but his friend begged him to use the whip. He preferred to be beaten than to lose his beloved prophet.

No matter how hard or how many times Hood ؊ hit the believing slave, no harm was done. No scars, nor pain, nor sign appeared on the body of the humble slave even though the blows were enough to kill a normal man. It was a miracle, and although the people of Ad took no notice and did not change, Allah's word must prove true against them.

Now they laughed at Hood ﷺ and left him alone. When the king heard Hood ﷺ teach about the Paradise gardens he decided to build himself a garden just to show the people that their heaven was really with him on earth. For twenty years the slaves labored to build this beautiful garden which was called Iram.

Now the king of Ad and his people became even more proud and boastful. They felt they were better than everyone else. While the rest of Arabia was covered with dry deserts, they lived in luxury in a fruitful garden. Just when their pride seemed to reach its height Allah Almighty stopped the rain. For seven years no rain fell. The crops withered. The flocks died. The people starved. Only the slaves were unchanged because they had gotten used to living on very little, and because their Prophet Hood ﷺ lived among them and the light that streamed from him gave them energy and hope.

The king of Ad made all his people pray to their gods for rain. On the horizon three clouds appeared. The first was white and out of it a voice spoke saying, "Choose me, I will rain snakes and scorpions upon you." The second was red and it said, "Choose me. I will rain fire upon you." The third was black and it said, "Choose me. I will rain a scorching wind upon you." However, no one but the believers could understand their words.

The people of Ad chose the black cloud because they were sure it looked like a rain cloud. Hood ﷺ begged them to listen to him, to listen to the True

God Who made them and Who could still save them. But they were sure now, in their pride, that the rain they had asked for had come and they chased Hood ﷺ away.

Hood ﷺ took the believers to the cave in the hills and covered the opening with stones and together they prayed.

The black cloud came closer and closer. The people who were at first so happy to see this cloud now began to be afraid. For seven nights and seven days a scorching wind attacked the people of Ad. The wind burned their bodies and melted their golden possessions. Great bird-like creatures came out of the cloud and tore the people to pieces and ripped their palaces from the ground and threw them about like bits of dust.

When it was over nothing remained of Ad, no house, no palace, no tree, no blade of grass. But the beautiful garden of Iram, because it was built by believers, was saved and hidden by Allah until on the Last Day it will appear again. Sometimes a believer, traveling alone in the desert, by Allah's permission, stumbles into this beautiful garden. But no matter how hard he searches he can never find it again.

Hood ﷺ took the believers and left that desolate place. They settled in the area of Mecca where at 150 years Hood ﷺ died and was buried near what would come to be the Ka'aba.

May Allah bless Hood ﷺ and give him peace.

Salih ﷺ

This is Allah's she-camel - a sign for you. So leave her alone to pasture in Allah's earth, and do her no harm. (7:73)

6

And the Light Passed to Salih علیه السلام

Two hundred years after the destruction of the people Ad some of their descendants again traveled north in Arabia with their leader whose name was Thamood. They were strong and unjust like their great grandfathers before them. They found a peaceful village whose people gave food and water to caravans and travelers. Thamood killed all the men and took the women captive and began living in their houses. Instead of feeding and serving tired travelers they killed them and took their possessions. Thamood became rich and powerful by killing and stealing.

To one of their chieftains was born a son in the line of the Prophet Hood علیه السلام. At his birth the light was so bright that even those forgetful people could see it and be amazed. The light of Muhammad ﷺ shone from the forehead of the baby like the sun bursting through an opening in the rocks. They named him Salih علیه السلام because, unlike his people, he was gentle and rightly guided.

Salih علیه السلام became an orphan early in his childhood and although he was raised as a future chieftain his people saw right away that he was different. He, like Hood علیه السلام, felt more at home among the slaves than among his lazy and hard-hearted relatives. He knew that a man is only as good as his heart whether or not he owns great wealth or has much power.

After forty years the Archangel Jibrail ﷺ appeared to Salih ﷺ out of a dense fog and brought the word from Allah that He had chosen Salih ﷺ as His Prophet. Salih ﷺ must now go out among the people to teach and show them by example the right way.

The people of Thamood were horrified that their future king lived as a poor man and a friend of the slaves. They decided he must be crazy to give up the best of this life, which was his inheritance. Many of the poor and the young, however, listened to Salih's ﷺ message and followed him. But many more of the people of Thamood turned against him. Salih ﷺ built a mosque in the mountains for his followers to pray in safety.

Finally at a yearly festival, Salih ﷺ gathered the many believers behind him and addressed the crowds of partygoers. He told them about their Lord, Who had created them from His Light, Who wanted only the best for them, and Who had sent him as a prophet to lead them to the path of goodness and happiness. They began to listen and the words of the prophet began to make sense. Salih's ﷺ speech was so beautiful that the forgetful people almost remembered who they were and from where they had come.

But there were nine very evil people among the Thamood. One of them shouted for Salih ﷺ to prove his prophethood by showing them a miracle. Now it is never a good idea to demand a miracle from the Lord. It is disrespectful and requires a commitment that once the miracle is witnessed the people will believe. So only after much argument did Salih ﷺ agree to ask his Lord for a miracle.

To the people of Thamood a camel was the most expensive and desirable possession. Only the wealthy could afford to own camels. A young female, able to produce many babies and gallons of good sweet milk for its owner, was the very best kind of camel. So the people of Thamood demanded that Allah create a young, beautiful, female camel from a large, worthless boulder that lay near the meeting place.

Salih ﷺ prayed and Allah answered his prayer. The large boulder split open like a cracked egg and a beautiful red camel stepped out, full grown, pregnant and swollen with milk. The people gasped in surprise but the nine evil men quickly shouted that it was just a trick designed to fool them. The people listened to these words and turned away from Salih ﷺ.

Allah gave them one more chance. Allah told Salih ﷺ to tell the people that no punishment would come if they respected the camel and left her free to graze and drink as she wanted. The people obeyed for a while. The camel gave birth to her child and had so much milk that the poor and hungry could always drink their fill. The rich people began to complain. The camel of Salih ﷺ, they said, drinks all our water and eats our grass and all her milk goes to the poor and worthless. Finally they could stand it no longer.

The nine evil men agreed to put an end to the problem. They decided to kill Salih ﷺ and the believers in their beds while they slept. After that they intended to cut the legs of the camel so that she could no longer walk to get food or drink and would die of starvation.

Salih ﷺ gathered his companions in the mosque and, by Allah's command, kept them there all night doing prayers and dhikr. The evil men did not find any of the believers and so killed none of them. They did, however, find the mother camel and they cruelly killed her. But they were not able to find the baby camel. Allah protected it by ordering the boulder to open again just long enough for the baby to slip inside. Then the rock closed forever, leaving no trace.

Now Allah told Salih ﷺ to take the believers and leave the country of Thamood. After they had left, Thamood rejoiced because they thought that they had won a victory over Salih ﷺ. They drank and danced until late in the night.

The next morning they awoke and found their faces had turned bright red. The following day their faces turned saffron yellow and the third day, jet black. They began to feel a terrible fear. As the sun rose on the fourth day the Archangel Jibrail ﷺ let out a mighty shout and the Earth began to tremble and shake as if it was made of water. For three days the people of Thamood were tossed about on the Earth like dry sticks on an angry ocean. The sky rained fire and the mountains fell into the valleys. On the seventh day when the sun rose not a stone remained standing of the fine houses of Thamood and not a single person was left alive.

Salih ﷺ took his people back to the site where the Ka'aba would later be built. There they settled in a new town in which Salih ﷺ lived peacefully until he was two hundred years old.

May Allah bless Salih ﷺ and give him peace.

Ibrahim ﷺ

We (Allah) said: Oh fire be coolness and peace for Ibrahim. (21:69)

7

And the Light Passed to Ibrahim ﷺ

After the Prophet Salih ﷺ had passed away, his people spread out from Arabia along the major river valleys to the East and West, along the Euphrates and the Nile. They built great cities and for a long time they kept their Islam strong. But as is the way with mankind, little by little they began to forget until they were as ignorant as their great-grandfathers had been. The most astray of all were the people of Nimrod the king. They worshipped him as a god and let him do and take whatever his evil desires dictated.

This Nimrod was very misguided. He married any woman he wanted regardless of her feelings and he killed any man who displeased him. One night he had a terrible nightmare in which he saw a bright star fall from the sky and land on his head. His counselors told him it meant a boy would be born who would replace him as king. Nimrod decided to kill every boy child that was born or would be born in the next ten years to any woman in his kingdom.

One of Nimrod's servants, Azar by name, carved wooden idols with the face of Nimrod for the people to worship. Azar's wife was pregnant. He quickly ran to tell her to hide herself and try to save the baby. She fled alone into the wilderness and soon became lost. All of a sudden she saw a beautiful being of light descend from the sky. It was the angel Jibrail ﷺ. He led her to a cave furnished like a palace with rugs and pillows and attended by heavenly servants. She safely delivered her baby, a little boy. He was very beautiful and she saw that from his forehead shone a light that lit up the cave and reached all the way to the heavens. She named him Ibrahim ﷺ.

After she had recovered the angel guided her home. But every night she returned to the cave and her infant son. One night she found the entrance to the cave blocked by a pack of wild animals. She became afraid for her son's life. But the animals spoke and told her to be calm. They had only come to see the Prophet of God, and they moved aside to let her enter. Inside she found her baby sucking his fingers. When she pulled out his hand in order to nurse him she found that from his first finger flowed butter, from his second honey, from his third rose water, from his fourth syrup, and from his fifth milk. He grew faster than other babies and in no time he was quite big.

For ten years Ibrahim ﷺ remained in the cave and saw no people other than his mother, and nothing of the world other than the inside of the cave. Finally he asked to see the world. His mother led him outside the cave into a night full of stars sparkling in the vast sky around him. "Oh Mother, what are those?" asked Ibrahim ﷺ in wonder. His mother answered him in her ignorance, "Those are gods, my son". But he saw the stars cross the sky and disappear behind the mountain and he said, "These do not remain. They cannot be God".

He saw the bright full moon rise in the sky and he asked his mother.

Again she replied, "That is God." Ibrahim ﷺ watched it until dawn when it too set behind the mountain. He told her "That is not God if it disappears."

Then he saw the sun rise big and red on the horizon. "That must be God," he said. All day he watched it cross the sky until it too disappeared behind the mountain. Then Ibrahim ﷺ understood that his parents and his people were mistaken. They knew nothing of God and he turned his heart directly to Allah Almighty and asked for help.

Jibrail ﷺ began to teach the young Ibrahim ﷺ about the Truth of things. When he was sixteen and it was safe, Ibrahim's ﷺ parents took him from the cave into town and introduced him as a visiting relative. Ibrahim ﷺ began to teach everyone who came to his father's idol shop about the one true God, Allah. Some people listened. Others just thought he was crazy. His mother believed, but his father began to lose business and became angry.

One day when all the people were at a festival for Nimrod, Ibrahim ﷺ took an axe and chopped all but one of the idols into pieces. When they returned the people were horrified and afraid. They grabbed Ibrahim ﷺ and questioned him. He blamed the deed on the largest statue which he had left standing. They knew that statues cannot use axes and they became confused. Ibrahim ﷺ then asked his people, "Why do you worship what can neither help nor hurt you?"

In anger Nimrod arrested him and put him in prison. He sentenced Ibrahim ﷺ to burn in a great fire as punishment. They gathered a mountain of firewood and put Ibrahim ﷺ in its center. The fire burned so hot that for miles away people had to shield themselves from the heat of its flames.

The animals tried to save Ibrahim ﷺ. Even the tiny bee carried a drop of water in its mouth to put out the flames. Allah gave the bee honey as a reward for its kindness. The birds and the wild beasts all prayed for his safety. The angels in heaven also begged Allah to save him. But Ibrahim ﷺ himself turned only to Allah and accepted whatever would come.

When after many days the fires burned down, through the smoke the people saw Ibrahim ﷺ sitting in prayer, unhurt and shining. Inside the burning mountain of fire Allah had made a paradise, green and cool for Ibrahim ﷺ.

After this Nimrod let Ibrahim ﷺ go. Ibrahim ﷺ left his parents and their unbelieving people. He gathered the believers around him and moved away from the lush river valleys and into the desert.

May Allah bless Ibrahim ﷺ and give him peace.

Ismail ﷺ

Oh my father do as you are commanded; if Allah please you will find me patient. (37:102)

8

And the Light Passed to Ismail ﷺ

Ibrahim ﷺ left everything of his father's behind him, his father's gods, his wealth, and his protection. He took only his beautiful believing wife, Sara ﷺ, and the believers, including his uncle's son, Lut ﷺ. They began to herd sheep and goats in the poor pastures of the Egyptian desert. But Allah increased Ibrahim ﷺ in everything and soon he was master over vast flocks of animals and large numbers of believers who followed him as their Prophet. Allah increased them all in children and grandchildren. Only Ibrahim ﷺ and Sara ﷺ had no children of their own, and they were growing old.

So one day Sara ﷺ, inspired by the Lord, asked Ibrahim ﷺ her husband to take as a second wife her believing slave, Hajar ﷺ, who had been given to her by the king of Egypt. Hajar ﷺ was young and beautiful and one of the grandchildren of Salih ﷺ. Sara ﷺ hoped she would bring children for Ibrahim ﷺ and their family would be complete.

But soon after the marriage of Ibrahim ﷺ and Hajar ﷺ Sara ﷺ became jealous. She could no longer stand the sight of Hajar ﷺ. Whenever she saw her she would try to hurt her, hoping Hajar ﷺ would run away. But Hajar ﷺ

was told by Allah to keep patience and she did not run. Sara ☪ became more and more jealous, more and more angry. She pierced holes in Hajar's ☪ ears and in her nose, which we still do today in memory of Hajar's ☪ patience. But Hajar ☪ remained steadfast. Ibrahim ☪ prayed for a son and promised Allah that he would sacrifice what he loved most should his prayer be granted.

Finally Hajar ☪ became pregnant and gave birth to a baby boy who they named Ismail ☪. When Sara ☪ saw the light streaming from the forehead of the baby she could stand no more. "Take them far away" she begged Ibrahim ☪. Hajar ☪ also wanted to leave and finally the Lord granted their prayer.

Ibrahim ☪ was told by an angel to put Hajar ☪ and Ismail ☪ on a camel and to take them into the desert. Where the camel stopped there he should leave them. The camel stopped at a desolate place in the rocky waterless hills of Tihama. Ibrahim ☪ obeyed his Lord. He kissed his wife and infant son and sadly turned and left them alone in a place where no thing lived.

For a few days Hajar ☪ and Ismail ☪ lived off the food and water they had brought with them. When it ran out Hajar ☪ became nervous. Ismail ☪ was crying. She ran from one hill to another. From the hill Safa to the hill Marwa she ran desperately looking for something to eat or drink.

Six times she ran and on the seventh time she saw Ismail blue in the face and kicking at the ground with his little heels. Where his right foot hit the ground the sand began to look dark and damp. Hajar ☪ lifted Ismail ☪ and scooped away the sand, building a small basin which filled quickly with cool, sweet water.

Hajar ☪ heard a voice from the well which said: "This is Zam Zam. If you are thirsty, drink and your thirst will be quenched. If you are hungry, drink and your hunger will be satisfied. If you are sick, drink and your sickness will be healed." She drank and gave to Ismail ☪.

Alone they lived by this well of Zam Zam for some time. One day a caravan, lost in the desert, stumbled upon them. The people drank and were healed and decided to stay by this miraculous well in the company of the humble mother and the beautiful child whose forehead shone like the moon on still waters. A town grew up around them which came to be called Mecca. Once a year Ibrahim ☪ would come to visit.

However, Ibrahim ☪ had made a promise to his Lord that he would sacrifice what was most dear to him and a promise must be kept. One night he had a dream that that sacrifice was to be Ismail ☪ his son. Seventy times Allah sent that dream to Ibrahim ☪. Sixty nine times Ibrahim ☪ tried to sacrifice something else, sheep, camels, horses, anything else. But finally after the seventieth dream Ibrahim ☪ took his rope and his knife and set out for Hajar's ☪ house.

Ibrahim ☪, his heart heavy with grief, asked Ismail ☪ to come with him for a walk. Together they followed the valley of Mina to the plain of Arafat, Ismail ☪ playfully skipping by his father's side. Three times Shaytan tried to tell Ismail that his father planned to kill him. Three times Ismail told Shaytan to go away: Whatever his father planned to do Ismail ☪ knew was the Will of Allah.

They came to a stop by a big rock and Ibrahim ﷺ told Ismail ﷺ his dream. His little son said, "Father, tie my hands so that I do not defend myself. Cover my face so we cannot see each other and turn me around so your heart does not break looking at me." Ibrahim ﷺ did all these things. Seventy times he steeled his heart and tried to sacrifice Ismail ﷺ. Seventy times the knife would not cut.

Only then did Allah send a sheep from heaven and tell Ibrahim ﷺ to sacrifice it in place of his son. Ibrahim's ﷺ promise had been kept. His trial was over. No man before or since has been tested as severely as Ibrahim ﷺ. We are ordered by Allah to remember the obedience of Ibrahim ﷺ and Ismail ﷺ on Eid al-Adha when we sacrifice a sheep as they did.

Later Ismail ﷺ and Ibrahim ﷺ were instructed by Allah to build Allah's Holy House on earth. This House is a reflection of The Holy House in Paradise. We call it the Ka'aba and it was first put on earth in the time of Adam ﷺ, but it was destroyed in the flood of Nuh ﷺ and forgotten.

Jibrail ﷺ showed them the spot on which to build by shadowing the sacred area with his wings and he brought the black stone to set in its corner. This stone had been white when it was sent from Paradise. It turned black from the sins of man. It was the only part of the original House to remain on earth after the flood by being protected in the depths of Mount Qubays. Mount Qubays was then honored by having its stones used to build the Holy House.

When it was completed Ibrahim ﷺ taught Ismail ﷺ how to perform the pilgrimage. Ibrahim then called out from each corner of the Ka'aba inviting the unseen people of the future to come and perform the pilgrimage. To this day the pilgrims are still answering Ibrahim's ﷺ call. Coming from all the corners of the earth they chant: "Here I come, oh Lord, here I am."

Ismail ﷺ grew to manhood and married a believing girl from among those who settled near Zam Zam. They had many good sons and grandsons to carry the light of Muhammad ﷺ but none of them were great prophets themselves. However, many years later in the city of The Holy House near the well of Zam Zam, a great-grandson of Ismail ﷺ would father the Prophet for whom the light was ultimately destined, the Prophet Muhammad ﷺ.

May Allah bless Ismail ﷺ and give him peace.

Lut ﷺ

We (Allah) turned them upside down and rained on them stones...
marked by your Lord with names. (11:82-83)

9

And the Light Passed to Lut ﷺ

Ibrahim ﷺ left his parents and his home and went into the desert accompanied by the believers, including the young son of his uncle whose name was Lut ﷺ. They left all they knew and trusted in Allah alone to provide for them and guide them. They left the company of the unbelievers to go into the desert and worship in the way they knew was right. And Allah increased them in all the good things of the material world and the spiritual world.

One day Ibrahim ﷺ saw in Lut's ﷺ face a great change. From his forehead shone a light like the pure glow of the moon on still water. Ibrahim ﷺ asked his nephew about it. Lut ﷺ replied that he had indeed received a visit from Jibrail ﷺ the night before informing him that he had been chosen by Allah to be one of His prophets.

At this time prophets were sent only to one particular people to teach them and guide them. To each people Allah sent a different prophet suited particularly for them. Lut ﷺ was ordered to leave his uncle and to travel north to the area of three cities close to Jerusalem.

The people of these cities were as ignorant and full of darkness as Lut ﷺ was guided and full of light. The men turned to other men for partners rather than to women. They left the girls unmarried and courted the boys. What Allah liked they shunned and what He hated they pursued. No prophet before or since has been sent to a more misguided, misbehaving, mixed up people.

Lut ﷺ traveled there alone without wife or family, friend or helper. He took one of their daughters to be his wife and settled down. He built a house. He worked in the fields. He became the best husband and neighbor. His wife bore him four beautiful daughters. But the people learned nothing from his good example. Even his wife did not become a believer.

Good and evil for these people were reversed. No matter what Lut ﷺ did or said they turned away and continued in their hurtful ways. Many times Lut ﷺ went to visit his uncle Ibrahim ﷺ in despair and each time Ibrahim ﷺ counseled patience and sent him back.

One day three travelers arrived at his house. In truth they were angels who had just come from visiting his uncle Ibrahim ﷺ. But to Lut ﷺ and the people of the city they looked like three young and handsome men who had lost their way and were without protectors. Lut ﷺ was afraid for their safety. The people of the city would steal their property and take them captive and Lut ﷺ was not strong enough to protect them.

Lut ﷺ tried to hide them by night in his house but his wife betrayed them. Men gathered outside the house of Lut ﷺ and began banging on the door. "Give us the beautiful boys" they cried.

Lut ﷺ begged them to leave the travelers alone. But the people had no shame and no mercy. Lut ﷺ even offered his four lovely daughters in marriage if the people would leave the strangers in peace. But they laughed at Lut ﷺ and intended to take what they wanted by force.

The three young men informed Lut ﷺ that they were really angels bringing Allah's punishment to the cities. They ordered Lut ﷺ to gather his family and the very few men and women who believed and leave the cities without looking back. Allah's anger and destruction were upon them.

Lut ﷺ did as he was commanded. As they climbed the hills above the city they heard a terrible noise and the air filled with smoke. Lut's ﷺ wife looked back in longing for her people and she was hit by a coal from hell and turned to stone. Hurriedly the believers followed the trail leading away from the cities.

Allah rained down on those unbelieving people live coals straight from the fires of hell. On each glowing coal was written the name of the person it was ordered to punish. The sky glowed red until it was hidden in the smoke of burning. Each person was hit by the coal with his name on it and died in great suffering. The angels turned the three cities upside down and buried them beneath the sand. The pit where they lay filled with water. The rocks of hell dissolved in it to make a sea so salty and bitter that no living thing could grow or survive near its bank or within its depths. This sea is called the Dead Sea and is without life to this day because it was the place of Allah's punishment.

Allah does not destroy a people out of anger. Even His punishment is out of Love. If the people cannot learn from words and example then they must be taught by discipline and punishment. But when they do learn and believe, even if only with their dying breath, they will be happy forever after.

Lut ﷺ and his daughters and the believers left the cities far behind them and rejoined other believers to live out their lives in peace and thankfulness.

May Allah bless Lut ﷺ and give him peace.

Ishaq ﷺ

We (Allah) give you good news of a boy possessing knowledge. (15:53)

10

And the Light Passed to Ishaq ﷺ

The angels disguised as three handsome men made a stop at the tents of Ibrahim ﷺ before they journeyed on to the cities of Lut ﷺ with news of the coming punishment. Allah had made Ibrahim ﷺ wealthy in all things. He had large numbers of sheep, goats and camels. He had beautiful tents and rugs. He traded for flour and olives and food of all kinds. He had friends and followers in all directions.

With all these gifts he had been given by his Lord Ibrahim ﷺ was most generous. He had guests come from far and wide to taste his hospitality. There was no man anywhere whose kindness and generosity were more legendary. He would not sit down to dinner without at least one guest to share his meal and usually he had many.

One evening, however, he found at his door these three travelers. They accepted his offer of shelter but they refused his food and drink. No matter how sweet and tasty, they took not one bite. Ibrahim ﷺ became afraid of them and wondered what harm they intended him because they would not share his food.

Then they revealed that they were angels and intended no harm but could not eat bread and meat like the children of Adam ﷺ. They had been sent by Allah to announce to Ibrahim ﷺ and Sara ﷺ the birth of a son. Now Ibrahim ﷺ was one hundred years old and Sara ﷺ was over eighty and they had had no children together and had given up hope of ever having any. On hearing this remarkable news Sara ﷺ laughed out loud in disbelief. But, sure enough, nine months later, Sara ﷺ gave birth to a baby boy whom they named Ishaq ﷺ, meaning she laughed.

Sara ﷺ and Ibrahim ﷺ were overjoyed. The light of Muhammad ﷺ shone from the brow of Ishaq ﷺ like the bright headlight of a long train traveling through the darkness.

Ishaq ﷺ grew into manhood and looked just like his father Ibrahim ﷺ. At this time there existed no signs of aging so the people had no way to tell father from son. Allah gave Ibrahim ﷺ gray hairs as a sign of his dignity and honor and to distinguish him from Ishaq ﷺ.

Ishaq ﷺ married a believing girl named Rifqa ﷺ. They herded the flocks for Ibrahim ﷺ and took over his guesthouse when he died. And Allah gave them wealth and many followers. Every year they made the pilgrimage to Mecca and visited with Ismail ﷺ and his family. Their oldest son married his cousin, the daughter of Ismail ﷺ.

Rifqa ﷺ had two more sons and they were born as twins. Even while still in the womb people could hear the boys arguing loudly. The first born was large and strong. They named him 'As ﷺ and his father loved him best.

The second born was slender and delicate. They named him Ya'qub ﷺ and he was his mother's favorite.

They grew to manhood as opposite in character as they had been born. 'As ﷺ was a fighter and a hunter. He was fierce and fearless. He hunted lions in the wilderness and tamed them to his will. He was large and covered with hair. Ya'qub ﷺ, however, was a shepherd. He spent his days guarding the sheep from wolves, and meditating on the wonders of Allah. He was gentle by nature and small in size.

When Ishaq ﷺ was dying he asked Rifqa ﷺ his wife to bring to him his son 'As ﷺ so that he could bless him and pass on to him the Ark and the gifts of prophethood. But Rifqa ﷺ intended these for Ya'qub ﷺ. She called Ya'qub ﷺ and told him to slaughter a sheep, bring the meat to his father and cover himself with the sheepskin and pretend to be 'As ﷺ. Ya'qub ﷺ did as his mother instructed him.

Ishaq ﷺ in old age had become blind. He hugged Ya'qub ﷺ and felt the fur and thought it was 'As ﷺ. He ate some of the meat and then, placing his hands on Ya'qub's ﷺ head, he blessed him with the blessing he intended for 'As ﷺ. Ishaq ﷺ prayed that his son might be the father of a long line of prophets. And this came to be. All the following prophets descend from Ishaq ﷺ except one and that one is the last Prophet, Muhammad Mustapha ﷺ.

Quickly Rifqa ﷺ told her son to run and hide. She knew that when 'As ﷺ discovered the deception he would try to kill his brother Ya'qub ﷺ. Ya'qub

ﷺ hid and, traveling only at night, made his way to relatives far to the south.

'As ﷺ returned in the evening and found his inheritance stolen. Ishaq ﷺ still had a blessing to give him but 'As ﷺ in his anger refused it, vowing to kill his brother and take back what he mistakenly thought was his rightful inheritance. He was mistaken because it is not possible for an undeserving person to steal such a thing as prophethood from Allah. Ya'qub ﷺ was the one for whom it was always intended.

May Allah bless Ishaq ﷺ and give him peace.

Ya'qub ﷺ

And he turned away from them and said: Oh my sorrow for Yusuf. (12:84)

II

And the Light Passed to Ya'qub ﷺ

The light shone from Ya'qub's ﷺ brow as it had from his father's. He fled from the revenge of his brother into the desert. At night he traveled. In daylight he hid in cracks and crevices. This flight by night is called *isra* in Arabic. So Ya'qub ﷺ was given the name Israil and his children and their children were called Banu Israil, the children of the one who takes flight by night.

When Ya'qub ﷺ reached safety at his uncle's tent in Madian he saw a young girl drawing water at the well. Even though she was quite young he fell in love with her. Her name was Raheel ﷺ and she was his uncle's daughter. Ya'qub ﷺ asked his uncle to marry her and they came to an agreement. Ya'qub ﷺ would work as a shepherd for his uncle for seven years, then he would be allowed to marry Raheel ﷺ.

At the end of seven years his uncle married Ya'qub ﷺ to his daughter. When the wedding veil was lifted Ya'qub ﷺ saw that it was the older daughter, Leah ﷺ, to whom he had been married, not Raheel ﷺ. At this time men were permitted to marry sisters, but naturally the oldest girl must be married first. So Ya'qub ﷺ worked for his uncle another seven years and finally was given

Raheel ؏ as his wife.

Ya'qub ؏ had eleven sons and many daughters, but he loved Yusuf ؏, the son of Raheel ؏, the most, because the light of Muhammad ﷺ shone like the morning star on his brow. It shone also from his other sons but not with the same brightness.

After some time, word came to Ya'qub ؏ that his father Ishaq ؏ and mother Rifqa ؏ had both died. He longed to visit their grave. Ya'qub ؏ packed up his tents and gathered his herds and set out for his homeland, although he knew his brother, 'As ؏, would still be seeking revenge. On the journey home his beloved wife Raheel ؏ died while giving birth to a second son, Benyameen ؏.

Ya'qub ؏ told all his sons to go ahead of him one at a time. He told them to look for their uncle 'As ؏. When they saw him they should reply to his questions by saying, "I am the child of a slave who has run from his master and who is returning to ask for forgiveness."

So one by one the sons of Ya'qub ؏ entered their uncle's land. And one by one they answered as they had been instructed. At first 'As ؏ was puzzled. Then he understood that his brother was approaching, and the desire for revenge raged in his heart. But little by little, as each child repeated his message of peace, the anger in the heart of 'As ؏ lessened. When Ya'qub ؏ himself finally appeared 'As ؏ ran to meet him. They embraced and 'As ؏ forgave Ya'qub ؏ with all his heart. He accepted that the inheritance had passed to Ya'qub ؏ by Allah's Will, not by deceit. 'As ؏ bowed down to Allah and welcomed Ya'qub ﷺ and shared with him all that he had. In this way Ya'qub ﷺ lost a beloved wife but regained a loving brother.

Ya'qub ﷺ stayed in the land of his father and raised his family. Ten of his sons grew strong and became shepherds. They went out every day with the flocks. But Ya'qub ﷺ kept Yusuf ﷺ at home where he could watch him and gaze at his beauty and the marvelous light that streamed from him.

The older brothers became jealous. They envied the love their father showered on their younger brother. But they envied most the light that Yusuf ﷺ carried. A heart that envies is open to the devil, and soon the brothers made a plan to get rid of Yusuf ﷺ, once and for all.

They begged their father to let them take Yusuf ﷺ with them one day to play in the meadows. Ya'qub ﷺ was reluctant but after much argument he allowed Yusuf ﷺ to go. Once in the meadows, far from their father's gaze, the brothers fell upon Yusuf ﷺ, tore his clothes and threw him down a deep well. Jibrail ﷺ caught him at the bottom by Allah's command so that he was not hurt.

Yusuf's ﷺ brothers took his shirt and soaked it in the blood of a bird they had killed and went running back to Ya'qub ﷺ. They told him they had left Yusuf ﷺ alone for only a few minutes and a wolf had come down from the mountains and eaten him. Ya'qub ﷺ knew they were lying but he knew also that by Allah's Will Yusuf ﷺ was gone, and he cried in fear and longing for his beloved son.

Every day the brothers returned to the well with small morsels of food which they fed Yusuf ﷺ until one day a caravan arrived. Drawing water from the well they discovered a beautiful boy. When they drew Yusuf ﷺ out of the well it was as if the sun had risen over the mountain. It was by this light that the brothers knew that Yusuf ﷺ was gone. The men of the caravan took Yusuf ﷺ with them to sell in a distant market as a slave.

May Allah bless Ya'qub ﷺ and give him peace.

Yusuf ﷺ

He said, no blame on you this day. May Allah forgive you. (12:92)

12

And the Light Passed to Yusuf ﷺ

The slave-traders knew they had a treasure when they pulled Yusuf ﷺ out of the well. They had never seen a boy so well formed and beautiful. Light radiated around him like the halo around the sun. It is said that Allah gave to Yusuf ﷺ ninety percent of all the beauty He had placed in the whole of creation.

So the slave-traders decided to take Yusuf ﷺ to Egypt in order to get the best price for him. They cleaned him up and dressed him well. A prince of Egypt saw him and determined to buy Yusuf ﷺ for his wife, Zulaykha ﷺ. If she liked they would adopt him, for they had no children of their own. He paid Yusuf's ﷺ weight in gold and took him home.

As they entered the house Zulaykha ﷺ gasped. When she was a child she had had a dream of this very same boy. She had been in love with him since that time. Her parents had married her to the aged Prince of Egypt against her will, but she had remained true to her love for Yusuf ﷺ. Now, here he was in front of her, a young child, who might even become her son. She went to her room and sobbed because there seemed no way out of her situation. She decided to keep her feelings secret and to wait.

They did not adopt Yusuf ﷺ but he grew to manhood in Zulaykha's ﷺ house, under her loving gaze. When he was grown into a handsome young man she was unable to control herself any longer. One day she reached for him, not as a mother, but as the lover she was in her heart. She was a beautiful woman and Yusuf ﷺ was terrified of doing something forbidden by Allah. He ran from her as she grabbed his shirt to hold him.

Zulaykha's ﷺ husband was outside the door and he heard the commotion. Zulaykha ﷺ tried to put the blame on Yusuf ﷺ but a servant advised the Prince that if he found Yusuf's ﷺ shirt torn in front, Zulaykha ﷺ was truthful. If, however, he found Yusuf's ﷺ shirt torn from behind, then Yusuf ﷺ was truthful. The shirt was torn from behind. The Prince grew angry with Zulaykha ﷺ and soon all the people of the city knew of her guilt and she felt great shame.

So Zulaykha ﷺ invited the women of the city to a luncheon at her house. At the end of the fine meal, she served them fruit and little knives with which to peel them. Just then Yusuf ﷺ entered the room. The ladies were so distracted by his great beauty that every one cut her fingers with the knife. They stopped speaking ill of Zulaykha ﷺ after that for they themselves could hardly resist the beauty of Yusuf ﷺ.

Yusuf ﷺ began to wear a veil over his face but the light of Muhammad ﷺ still sparkled around him. It became more and more difficult to live together in the same house. Yusuf ﷺ prayed to Allah to protect him from committing any sin. In answer to this prayer Allah had the men put Yusuf ﷺ in prison on account of the trouble his beauty caused among the women

Zulaykha ﷻ mourned his loss and became crazy with grief. Her husband died. She gave away all her wealth. Her beauty faded. She wandered the streets asking for any news of Yusuf ﷺ, but Yusuf ﷺ had been forgotten by everyone else.

In prison Yusuf ﷺ was content. He worshipped Allah in quiet and safety. His light brought happiness and hope to the wretched souls locked up with him. The guards loved him and took special care of him.

Allah gave Yusuf ﷺ the ability to interpret dreams. One day two prisoners presented to him their troubling dreams. He told them the meanings and both came true. One prisoner was executed and one was pardoned. The one set free became a servant to the King.

Many years later the King had a dream that greatly troubled him. He asked all his advisors to tell him the meaning, but they were unable to give a proper interpretation. Then the servant remembered Yusuf ﷺ. The King called for Yusuf ﷺ to be brought to him out of the prison.

By Allah's permission Yusuf ﷺ understood the King's dream. Egypt would have seven years of rain and good harvests followed by seven years of drought and famine. He counseled the King to put extra food in big storehouses for the first seven years, and then, for the next seven years, to distribute it little by little to the people to keep them from starvation. The King was very impressed by Yusuf's ﷺ understanding and by his counsel. He raised him out of the prison and made him chief advisor and guardian over the storehouses.

It came to pass just as Yusuf ﷺ had predicted. The seven years of plenty were followed by seven years of famine. People came from all over the region to buy food in Egypt because there was none to be had elsewhere. Among those coming for food, one day, Yusuf ﷺ saw familiar faces. They were those of his ten brothers who had thrown him down the well. He knew them but they did not recognize him.

He talked to them a little and asked about their circumstances. They told him they had left at home an old father who had become blind in weeping for a dead child and a little brother who the father kept constantly by his side as a reminder of the lost son. Yusuf ﷺ gave them generous portions of grain and asked them to return with their brother. They went home and begged their father Ya'qub ﷺ to let them take Benyameen ﷺ, their youngest brother, with them to Egypt. Ya'qub ﷺ was reluctant but in the end agreed.

All eleven of the sons returned to Egypt. Yusuf ﷺ gave them generous portions of grain but hid the King's golden cup in Benyameen's ﷺ bag. At the gate of the city the guards checked the bags and discovered the cup. Accusing Benyameen ﷺ of theft, they put him in jail. The brothers were very upset. Regret for their past actions surged inside them. How could they face their beloved father again with news that they had lost his dearest son? They tried to persuade Yusuf ﷺ to let Benyameen ﷺ go or at least to take one of them in his place. Yusuf ﷺ ordered them to leave and return quickly with their old father. He sent as a gift one of his own fine shirts.

When they had gone he revealed his true identity to Benyameen ﷺ. They embraced and went home to Yusuf's ﷺ palace.

The brothers hurried home, suffering great agonies at having to relive the past and break their father's heart again. They were afraid that the news of Benyameen's ﷺ imprisonment would kill Ya'qub ﷺ. But Ya'qub ﷺ, even before the brothers arrived, could smell the sweet scent of Yusuf ﷺ on the shirt they carried. They greeted him and presented him the gift of Yusuf's ﷺ shirt. He buried his face in it and his eyes regained their sight. Quickly they packed up all the tents and animals, women and children and made their way to Egypt.

When Ya'qub ﷺ and Yusuf ﷺ saw each other they fell to their knees for three hours unable to speak or move out of joy. All the people of Egypt and all the angels of Heaven were moved to tears. Then his brothers asked for forgiveness with all their hearts and Yusuf ﷺ forgave them. He invited them all to stay in Egypt where eventually Yusuf ﷺ became King and all his people followed him in worshipping the One True God.

But the story does not end there. One day while inspecting the city, Yusuf ﷺ came across an old crazy woman dressed in dirty rags. She begged him to ask Allah to grant her prayers. Yusuf ﷺ, in kindness, did what she asked. Suddenly the old woman became young again and beautiful. He recognized her as Zulaykha ﷺ. She became a believer and by Allah's Will she and Yusuf ﷺ were finally married. They had eleven sons and each of his brothers had twelve sons. They all had their own pastures and watering places and they continued to dwell together in the land of Egypt in peace and prosperity for many generations.

May Allah bless Yusuf ﷺ and give him peace.

Ayyoub ﷺ

Stamp with your foot. Here is cool water to wash with and to drink. (38:42)

13

And the Light Passed to Ayyoub ﷺ

In the village of Qudsiya near Damascus a son was born to descendants of the Prophets. His father, Mus, ﷺ was a descendant of the sons of Ya'qub ﷺ and his mother, Anoos ﷺ, was descended from the daughters of Lut ﷺ. They named their baby Ayyoub ﷺ and the light shone from his forehead with the steadiness of the moon on a clear night.

Ayyoub ﷺ grew to manhood and became wealthy. He owned many fine houses, orchards and gardens full of every kind of fruit and good thing to eat. He married Rahma ﷺ, a descendant of Yusuf ﷺ, and they had fifteen sons.

They lacked for nothing. Ayyoub ﷺ married two more wives and had more children and grandchildren. They all lived together in harmony and love. Every night they gathered in one of the houses and ate and worshipped together. Life was good to them.

In all this good fortune Ayyoub ﷺ never forgot to thank his Lord from Whom all things come. He was a humble servant to Allah and a generous neighbor to all. Allah had given him as much as He had given to any man and yet Ayyoub ﷺ never forgot his Creator. He was a model of a man.

One day Shaytan, the jealous one, could stand the good fortune of Ayyoub ﷺ no longer. He told the angels that Ayyoub ﷺ remembered Allah only because he had been given so much and had nothing to complain about. Allah gave Shaytan permission to test Ayyoub ﷺ.

The next day, while Ayyoub ﷺ was praying in the mosque, a great windstorm arose and destroyed his gardens and scattered his flocks. In one day all Ayyoub's ﷺ wealth was gone. Still he remained undistracted in the mosque praising and worshipping Allah.

The next day when all Ayyoub's ﷺ children and grandchildren were gathered together in one of his houses for dinner a great quake shook the earth. The roof fell and in one moment killed all Ayyoub's ﷺ children, their wives and their children.

This terrible calamity only increased Ayyoub ﷺ in patience and love for his Lord. He stayed in prayer and turned his eyes only to Allah. Shaytan was beside himself with fury. Allah and His angels praised the steady heart of Ayyoub ﷺ and knew that nothing could change him.

Then Shaytan blew at Ayyoub ﷺ a poisonous breath from Hell that made his body swell and break out in oozing sores. Shaytan then went house to house in the village telling the people that Ayyoub ﷺ must be corrupt to deserve such punishment. Even though the people of the village had respected and honored Ayyoub ﷺ, they had never given up their belief in idols. Only three strangers passing through had believed and followed Ayyoub ﷺ. Now his disease sickened the villagers and made them afraid. They lost respect for him altogether.

Two of Ayyoub's ﷺ wives left him. Only Rahma ﷺ remained. The men of the village thought he might be contagious so they made Rahma ﷺ carry Ayyoub ﷺ on her back far away into the wasteland that surrounded the village. There Rahma ﷺ made him a bed of dry grass, with a stone for a pillow. Nobody came to help them or give them comfort or food. Rahma ﷺ went searching for work in the village. She, who had been an elegant lady before, now did any dirty job that would bring enough food for herself and her husband.

Rahma ﷺ had been very beautiful with long hair that reached below her knees. Shaytan inspired one of the village women to insist on cutting Rahma's ﷺ hair in exchange for food. Short hair at that time was a sign of a woman who had broken the law. When Ayyoub ﷺ saw his wife's hair cut short he doubted her goodness and refused to believe the truth of her story. He swore to beat her if he ever regained his strength. Shaytan had almost destroyed every earthly thing of value to Ayyoub ﷺ, even the love and trust between husband and wife.

The three strangers who had accepted Ayyoub ﷺ as their prophet now reconsidered their decision. They began to doubt Ayyoub ﷺ and went back to worshipping idols. This was the final blow. With his heart burning in his chest Ayyoub ﷺ prayed to Allah to preserve His religion on earth, to save the believers from doubt and for the first time, Ayyoub ﷺ prayed for himself. He asked Allah to remember His servant Ayyoub ﷺ.

Allah answered his prayer, telling Ayyoub ﷺ to go into the wasteland and stamp his foot on the ground. Ayyoub ﷺ did as he was bidden. He dragged himself off his sickbed, struggled to his feet and stamped. In that dry, forsaken wasteland a fountain of water shot up beneath his feet. It bathed him in water. Ayyoub ﷺ became healthy, young and strong once more. When Rahma ﷺ returned from the village Ayyoub ﷺ had her also bathe in the fountain and she became young and beautiful again.

The three believers and all the people of the village witnessed this miracle and became believers. Everything that had been taken from Ayyoub ﷺ was restored. He was given more children and grandchildren, houses and gardens. People say that even the crickets in his gardens were made of gold. And Shaytan was driven from that land, shamed and despised.

A prophet must keep his promises and Ayyoub ﷺ had promised to beat Rahma ﷺ if he ever got well. Now, of course, he understood her innocence and did not want to hurt her. Allah ordered that Ayyoub ﷺ fulfill his vow by hitting Rahma ﷺ with soft grasses.

Ayyoub ﷺ lived to be two hundred and ninety years old. In bad times and good times he kept his heart turned towards his Creator, grateful and humble. Now Allah always knew the strength of heart of Ayyoub ﷺ, but He allowed Shaytan to test Ayyoub ﷺ in order to show all people everywhere that if a man is patient he will withstand and, in the end, triumph over any evil.

May Allah bless Ayyoub ﷺ and give him peace.

Dhul-Kifl

And remember Ismail and Alyasa' and Dhul-Kifl and they were all of the best ones. (38:48)

14

And the Light Passed to Dhul-Kifl ﷺ

Among the sons born to Ayyoub ﷺ and Rahma ﷺ after they were healed was one they name Bishr ﷺ on whose forehead they saw the light shine like a torch on a moonless night. He was a handsome youth with a friendly smile and easy ways. He wore his hair long and parted it in the middle and for this reason he was given the nickname, Dhul-Kifl ﷺ.

At the death of his father, Ayyoub ﷺ, all the people of Qudsiya and the surrounding villages were believers. The idols had been smashed and mosques built on every hill. The people were God-fearing and kind. Their contentment shone on their faces.

The king of the neighboring country began to feel jealous. The people of Ayyoub ﷺ must have uncountable treasures, he thought, to be so happy and contented. And he decided to invade Qudsiya with his army, make the people slaves and take their wealth.

But Dhul-Kifl ﷺ was warned of the coming attack and he and his brothers hid in the hills. They ambushed the invading army and took it captive. They invited the army to believe in Allah and live with them in peace but none of the soldiers understood how to worship a god they could not see.

The jealous king was furious at the loss of his army. He determined to use a more subtle method to destroy his enemy. He decided to corrupt the young people. He sent merchants to the city to tempt the young with fancy clothes and useless things. The merchants then introduced the young to drinking and dancing and gambling. These were the poisonous seeds planted by the enemy king in order to destroy the happiness of the believers.

The seeds grew in the hearts of the young people. They became ashamed and felt the need to lie to their parents about what they had done. They avoided prayers and the mosque, ashamed before Allah. They drank and gambled more. They needed money so they stole. This led to fighting and murder. Little by little their behavior worsened and their faith crumbled. Soon only the old were to be seen in the mosques.

Dhul-Kifl ﷺ tried to speak to the young people but they were full of drink and could no longer understand. They became angry and decided to solve the problem by killing the ones who reminded them of who they had been and made them feel ashamed of who they had become. They attacked Dhu-Kifl ﷺ and the believers. It was a terrible fight, father against son, mother against daughter. But by morning the old believers had won, because the young were drunk and had lost courage.

The young rebels fled the village and took refuge with the enemy king, who they thought was their friend. With their help the king planned to invade once again.

Dhul-Kifl ﷺ was ordered by Allah to take the believers and move to Damascus. Only forty of them were strong enough to leave their homes and fields and all their belongings to set out for a new land where they owned nothing.

On the road they met a messenger from Dhul-Kifl's ﷺ brother urging them to return to the village. He said the evil king was no longer intent upon invasion. The believers, homesick already, left their prophet Dhul-Kifl ﷺ in the middle of the road and returned to their village.

Dhul-Kifl ﷺ followed them secretly to see what would happen. The village was attacked and destroyed and its people sold into slavery. Dhul-Kifl ﷺ traveled on alone to Damascus.

There he married and built a house and had many children. One day he saw a slave caravan passing his house. The guards beat the slaves mercilessly. The slaves were starving and near death. For love of Allah Dhul-Kifl ﷺ bought the slaves who were too sick to be sold at the slave market anyway. As he fed them and gave them water they began to recover. Soon they recognized him as their prophet, for they were the young people of Qudsiya who had been betrayed by the enemy king and sold into slavery. They became believers again under their prophet, Dhul-Kifl ﷺ, and settled near him and married and had families.

The ruler of Damascus became suspicious of Dhul-Kifl ﷺ and ordered that the prophet leave the city. Dhul-Kifl ﷺ could not bear to uproot the slaves one more time. He bid them farewell and set out alone. Under Allah's Command Dhul-Kifl ﷺ traveled for many years. Wherever he went he spoke about Allah and showed the way to peace and happiness. He saw many strange people. He endured many hardships and had many adventures. He met people who lived in holes under ground, people who lived in ice and snow. Some listened to his message but most heard nothing.

Finally Allah allowed Dhul-Kifl ﷺ to return to his family in Damascus. His wife and his children rejoiced to see him. The slaves had held firmly to their renewed faith and they were overjoyed to see the return of their prophet.

Dhul-Kifl ﷺ continued to live and teach in Damascus until he was seventy-five. He died leaving no child able to bear the light of prophethood upon his brow.

May Allah bless Dhul-Kifl ﷺ and give him peace.

Shu'ayb ﷺ

Those who called Shu'ayb a liar, they were the losers. (7:92)

15

And the Light Passed to Shu'ayb ﷺ

Shu'ayb ﷺ was the great, great grandson of Ibrahim ﷺ. His name means, "The one whose heart is on fire with the love of God," and the glow from that fire shone from his face and lighted the world around him. He was sent to the people of Madian and given the gift of speaking beautifully and persuasively.

The people of Madian were merchants and store keepers. They cheated in all their business dealings and took advantage of the poor and the weak. Shu'ayb ﷺ scolded them and advised them against these practices, but they did not listen and eventually made him leave the city.

Shu'ayb ﷺ and the believers moved to the outskirts of Madian, and in the hills they built houses and pastured their sheep and goats. Still every day Shu'ayb ﷺ would stand outside the city gates, his staff in his hand, his long beard flowing, his face radiant with the love of God. In beautiful and powerful words he would warn the people and advise them to be honest and straight if they wished to avoid the punishment of Allah.

During this period a stranger came to Madian from Egypt. He was a descendant of prophets and the light of Muhammad ﷺ shone from his brow. He married Shu'ayb's ﷺ eldest daughter and became the son Shu'ayb ﷺ was hoping for.

But the people of Madian turned a deaf ear to the warnings of Shu'ayb ﷺ. They stoned him and one day made him move even farther from the city. The believers, and there were a good number of them, gathered around him. Shu'ayb ﷺ kept them in prayer all night until the sun rose on the terrible day the punishment of Allah descended on the stubborn people of Madian.

The sun heated up until the air was like a furnace and the earth like an oven. Nowhere could the unbelievers of Madian find coolness or shade. Their bodies felt as if they were on fire. They saw a cloud in the distance and ran for its shadow thinking it brought rain and relief. It brought only more fire. Sparks flew out of the cloud and burning embers. The unbelievers were consumed in the fire. The earth shook and swallowed the remains of the people and all their wealth and possessions, as if they had never been.

Shu'ayb ﷺ took the believers and traveled north to visit the sites of the earlier prophets. They visited the ark of Nuh ﷺ, the sea of Lut ﷺ, the place where Nimrod had tried to burn Ibrahim ﷺ. Then they traveled south past the ruins of the cities of Salih ﷺ and Hood ﷺ. Finally they came to the Ka'aba. There they drank the waters of Zam Zam and settled down. Shu'ayb ﷺ preached to the people in that area who had once again forgotten the Words of Allah. And most people believed and accepted him as their prophet.

Shu'ayb ﷺ lived in peace until he was 300 years old and died and was buried near the Ka'aba. He was succeeded, not by a son, but by his daughter's husband, Musa ﷺ.

May Allah bless Shu'ayb ﷺ and give him peace.

Musa ﷺ

Place him into an ark, then put it into the river. The river will bring it to shore. (20:39)

16

And the Light Passed to Musa ﷺ

In Egypt the children of Ya'qub ﷺ continued to live and prosper. However, little by little, the Egyptians had forgotten the God of Yusuf ﷺ and returned to worshipping false gods. In fact the king of Egypt, Pharaoh, began to be worshipped as a god himself. Then the children of Ya'qub ﷺ, who were called the Banu Israil, began to be mistreated and abused because they continued to believe in Allah, the Unseen Creator of all that is seen.

Although an idol worshipper, Pharaoh had been a good and a just leader until he realized that one day his kingdom and his power would come to an end. He became afraid of anyone who might oppose him. He feared the slaves because they had something to gain if he died. He feared the Banu Israil because they did not believe he was god. He had a dream that confirmed this fear. He determined to kill all the boy children of the Banu Israil so that they would never grow strong enough to harm him.

One granddaughter of Ya'qub ﷺ named Yohabith ﷺ lived up river from the Pharaoh's palace. Her daughter, Mariam ﷺ, worked for Queen Asiya ﷺ. Yohabith ﷺ also had a baby boy who she named Musa ﷺ, and the light of the Prophet Muhammad ﷺ shone from his forehead like a guiding star. To save him from Pharaoh, Yohabith ؑ was inspired by Allah to put Musa ؑ in a wooden box, an ark, and set him adrift on the river Nile. Although she was afraid for his safety she obeyed her inspiration. She sat by the river weeping as she watched the tiny ark float away with its precious cargo. Allah promised her that if she was patient the baby would be safely returned to her.

The little wooden ark floated downstream to where the Queen and her maidens were bathing. They swam out to the box and found the beautiful baby inside. Asiya ؑ the queen loved him immediately and took him to her husband, Pharaoh. They decided to adopt the baby. They put him under the care of Mariam ؑ, unaware that she was his sister, and she gave him back to his mother, Yohabith ؑ to nurse. It was as Allah had promised. Musa ؑ grew to manhood safely under the care of his own mother.

Yohabith ؑ had more children including another son named Harun ؑ. Musa ؑ grew up surrounded by his loving family. He was raised as the son of the king but he was fully aware that he was actually the son of slaves, and of prophets.

One day Musa ؑ came upon a soldier of the king beating a slave of the Banu Israil almost to death. Anger rose inside him at the sight of this unjust treatment. He only raised his hand to stop the beating and the soldier died instantly. Musa ؑ was still a young man and as yet unaware of the strength of his spiritual power and righteous anger. He had not meant to hurt the soldier, only to stop him.

Now he had to flee Egypt. Pharaoh would arrest anyone who killed one of his soldiers. Musa ﷺ left his two mothers, Yohabith ؇ and Asiya ؇ and fled across the sea to Arabia.

He traveled at night until he reached the neighborhood of Madian. There he rested by a well. In the morning he saw shepherds come to water their flocks. There were two young girls who waited nearby because they were too shy to mingle with the men at the well. Musa ﷺ offered to draw water for them. They were very thankful and ran to tell their old father about the kindness of the stranger.

Their father was the prophet Shu'ayb ﷺ and he saw the light shining from the face of the stranger. He offered Musa ﷺ his oldest daughter Zipporah ؇ in marriage and a job taking care of his sheep. Musa ﷺ accepted and came to live with Shu'ayb ﷺ as his son-in-law.

Shu'ayb ﷺ had been entrusted by Allah with a staff that had belonged to the first prophet Adam ﷺ. This he gave to Musa ﷺ. It was made from a tree of paradise, and had special powers.

Musa ﷺ lived many years with Shu'ayb ﷺ. Then one day he asked permission to take his wife and children to Egypt to visit his mother. They left Madian and set out across the Sinai to Egypt. It was winter and the desert was cold and without shelter. After many nights of fierce wind the small family lost their fire. Musa ﷺ saw a campfire burning in the distance. He left his family and set out to borrow some of the coals and to hear some news of Egypt from the people he thought he would find there.

When he got close to the campfire he saw a strange sight, a bush glowing with flames but itself untouched by fire. He heard a voice coming from the vicinity of this bush of intense light. It was Allah Almighty speaking directly to him. Musa ﷺ spent three days talking with Allah in that sacred place. Allah commanded him to return to Egypt and lead the believers to freedom and a land of their own. Musa ﷺ felt too small for such a large task and asked Allah if his brother Harun ﷺ could also be made a prophet to help him. Allah granted his wish and for the first time two brothers shared the prophethood together.

May Allah bless Musa ﷺ and give him peace.

Harun ﷺ

Then We sent Musa and his brother Harun with Our signs and a clear authority. (23:45)

17

And the Light Passed also to Harun ﷺ

Harun ﷺ from birth carried the light of Muhammad ﷺ but not the responsibility of guiding a people. That task was given to his brother Musa ﷺ. It was only at Musa's ﷺ request that Allah also gave Harun ﷺ the burden and honor of the prophethood. The two brothers complemented each other. Musa ﷺ was like a passionate flame while Harun ﷺ was like deep still water. Musa ﷺ acted boldly. Harun ﷺ spoke from an inner sweetness. It is from the descendants of Harun ﷺ that the priests of the Banu Israil are chosen.

Musa ﷺ and Harun ﷺ went to Pharaoh and tried to convince him that there is only one God, Allah, Who made all of creation and rules over it with Justice. Pharaoh refused to listen. For many years they patiently reasoned with him. But he only became more angry and proud. Other people, however, did listen.

Pharaoh ordered his wise men to challenge Musa ﷺ to a contest to see whose magic was stronger. The wise men threw their staffs to the ground and they became snakes slithering and sliding venomously towards Musa ﷺ. Musa ﷺ called on Allah's help and threw down his staff that had belonged to

Adam ﷺ. His staff became a huge dragon that ate all the snakes in one fiery gulp. The magic of men is no competition for the magic of Allah. The wise men understood and immediately became believers in the God of Musa ﷺ.

Pharaoh had his wise men tortured and killed. When Asiya ؓ his queen was discovered to be a believer he had her tortured also and killed. Their souls were taken to live forever in Heavenly mansions close to Allah.

Finally Musa ﷺ warned Pharaoh of Allah's punishment if he did not allow the believers to leave Egypt. Now Musa ﷺ used his staff to turn the river Nile into a river of blood. For eight days the people had nothing to drink and nowhere to wash. Still Pharaoh did not believe. Then a cloud of locusts came and ate all the crops. Then millions of frogs swarmed out of the swamps to eat the locusts. The farm animals got sick and died. There were freak hailstorms. There was famine. Many people became stricken with disease. Still Pharaoh and the people were proud and would not believe.

Finally Allah sent the Angel of Death ﷺ. Musa ﷺ told the believers to paint their doors with the blood of a sheep they had sacrificed to Allah. Any house not so marked the Angel entered and took the oldest child. There was death all over Egypt, in the huts and in the palaces.

While the Egyptians were distracted, mourning and burying their dead, Musa ﷺ and Harun ﷺ led the believers out of Egypt. They carried their belongings with them and moved slowly. Pharaoh and his army quickly caught up with them. The believers were trapped between Pharaoh's army and the sea. But Allah ordered Musa ﷺ to strike the sea with his staff. The waters opened up making walls on each side and exposing the floor of the sea like an open road. The believers followed their prophets through this opening to freedom. When Pharaoh tried to follow, the walls of water collapsed over him and his army. They all drowned.

Now the believers were free, but they had no home of their own. They camped in the desert while Musa ﷺ continued to talk with his Lord. He would climb the mountain near the glowing bush where he had first talked with Allah. There he would fast and pray. Allah would talk to him as to a beloved friend. Musa ﷺ talked to Allah but he longed to see Allah with his eyes. Finally Allah agreed saying He would reveal Himself to the mountain in plain view of where Musa ﷺ knelt. When the first Ray of Allah's Light struck the mountain it shattered into seven parts and crumbled into dust. Three of its stones would later become useful to another prophet, Daud ﷺ. From that day on Musa ﷺ wore a veil because the light on his face had become so intense that the believers could not look at him without being blinded.

Musa ﷺ was given the Holy Book, called the Torah, which was chiseled by Angels on slabs of stone. It told the people to worship Allah alone and to be thankful to Allah alone and respectful to their parents. They must never steal, or murder, or commit adultery. They must treat all men as they themselves would like to be treated. They must only sacrifice animals for food in Allah's name, quickly and mercifully. They must set aside one day a week for praying and on that day do no work of any kind.

While Musa ﷺ was on the mountain talking to God, Harun ﷺ continued to lead the people in prayer in the valley. They missed Musa ﷺ. It seemed their beloved Prophet spent all his time on the mountain, fasting and praying. When he returned to them he was veiled. They felt abandoned and homeless. They quickly lost patience with what they could not understand. They forgot the miracles Allah had performed in order to free them. They looked for something they could see and touch. Shaytan inspired them to make a statue of a cow out of gold. The people began to worship this cow. It reminded them of the milk and abundance and the security they had left behind in their homes in Egypt. Harun ﷺ argued and pleaded with them without success. Finally he and a few steadfast believers left and settled elsewhere.

When Musa ﷺ returned from the mountain with the Torah in his hands and saw what his people had done his anger knew no bounds. He threw the slabs to the ground. Many of the verses flew back to Heaven. What remained was broken. The people saw the anger of their prophet and they were sorry. They destroyed the golden cow and prayed for forgiveness.

Allah forgave them and promised them a land of their own. But when the Banu Israil arrived at the border of that land they saw it already occupied by a fierce warlike people. Although the Lord commanded it and they had prophets to lead them, the people were afraid. They refused to fight. They dared not enter the land that was promised them.

Allah punished them for their lack of faith by condemning them to wander, lost in the desert. Every morning they would set out looking for a place to settle down and every evening they would find themselves back in the place from which they had started. For forty years Allah led the Banu Israil in circles, until both their prophets Harun ﷺ and Musa ﷺ had died. Only two of all the men who had accompanied the prophets out of Egypt were left alive.

May Allah bless Musa ﷺ and Harun ﷺ and give them peace.

Yusha ﷺ

O my people enter the Holy Land which Allah has promised you. (5:21)

18

And the Light Passed to Yusha ﷺ

One of the original men who had followed Musa ﷺ and Harun ﷺ out of Egypt was Yusha ﷺ. He was just a child when he took Musa's ﷺ hand and became his servant. Yusha ﷺ served Musa ﷺ during all the events in Egypt. He stood by as the prophets tried to reason with Pharaoh. He witnessed the miracles and the plagues. Wherever Musa ﷺ went Yusha ﷺ followed.

At one time he accompanied Musa ﷺ south along the Nile to look for the wise man, Khidr ﷺ, from whom Musa ﷺ wished to learn. Musa ﷺ was told to carry a dry fish for his lunch and when the fish became alive and swam away into the river he would know Khidr ﷺ was near. It was Yusha ﷺ who carried the lunch for Musa ﷺ and who saw the miracle of the fish. Musa ﷺ then went off alone with Khidr ﷺ to learn and be tested while Yusha ﷺ waited patiently for his return.

Musa ﷺ and Khidr ﷺ were given a ride across the river in a small boat. The owner of the boat was very kind and charged them no money for the trip. Still when they landed on the far shore Khidr ﷺ, under cover of darkness, put a hole in the bottom of the boat. Musa ﷺ was horrified.

As they were traveling down the road they saw a group of small boys playing in the dirt. One boy in particular caught their eye with his sweet smile and friendly ways. Khidr ﷺ reached out his hand and struck the boy dead. Musa ﷺ could not contain his horror.

That night they rested in a village where no one offered them food or hospitality. The villagers were unfriendly and ungenerous. In the morning Khidr ﷺ made Musa ﷺ help him in repairing a stone wall that had begun to crumble.

Musa ﷺ could contain his disapproval no longer. He questioned Khidr's ﷺ actions. "Why did you destroy the boat of the generous man? Why did you kill an innocent child? Why did we work for the benefit of people who denied us even water?"

"We can no longer travel together. You are not able to learn from me," answered Khidr ﷺ. "A greedy king is coming who will take without payment any boat in good repair. I put a hole in the boat so that the king will not take it and the kind owner will be able to keep and repair it."

"The child I killed was the son of believers. He was destined to be a cruel criminal and cause his parents much pain. I took his life while he was still innocent and Allah Almighty will give his parents in his place many good and believing sons."

"As for the wall, it belonged to orphan children. Underneath it is buried a treasure their believing father left for them. If the wall falls before the children are grown the greedy villagers will steal their treasure and they will have nothing."

So Khidr ﷻ explained to Musa ﷻ the wisdom behind his mysterious actions. Khidr ﷻ acted on knowledge that only Allah could give him. Three lessons Khidr ﷻ gave Musa ﷻ and three tests. Musa ﷻ failed them all. The purpose was to teach all of us that however much we know there will always be someone who knows more. And however much we or even a great prophet know, what remains unknown and unknowable of Allah's vast Creation and Majesty is far, far greater.

Much later when Musa ﷻ went up the mountain to talk with Allah Yusha ﷻ still waited for him at the bottom. When the people built the golden cow Yusha ﷻ protested and then protected and helped Harun ﷻ. Always he was a faithful and obedient servant. Before he died Musa ﷻ was told by Allah to inform the Banu Israil that Yusha ﷻ would be their next prophet. He would be the one to lead them into the land that Allah had promised them.

Yusha ﷻ was eighty-two years old when Allah made him His prophet. For twenty-eight years he led the believers of the Banu Israil in establishing a country of their own, ruled by the Laws Allah had laid down in the Torah. Although he was getting old, he was still a strong and mighty warrior. He led his army across the Jordan River and vanquished kingdom after kingdom until he was in full control of all the land stretching from Damascus to the sea. After a long siege they took the city of Jerusalem also.

The Banu Israil established themselves in the land. Ya'qub ﷺ had had twelve sons; Yusuf ﷺ and Benyameen ﷺ from Raheel ؇ and ten sons from his first wife, Leah ؇. Allah commanded that the descendants of each of these brothers be given their own territory and watering places. So the land of Israil, as their country came to be called, was divided into twelve equal parts.

At first things went well. The Banu Israil respected their prophet and obeyed Allah. The conquered people were happy with their new rulers who treated them with mercy and justice. But little by little the believers became corrupted by the practices of their neighbors. They no longer kept Allah's Law. They gambled and partied. They began to fight among themselves. They forgot the misery their parents had endured as slaves of the Pharoah in Egypt, and they began to behave like Pharoah and to mistreat the conquered people. They took what they wanted without asking and quickly became tyrants in the land.

Yusha ﷺ in disgust retreated to the mountains to pray and worship Allah alone. He still went down into the cities frequently to remind and correct his people but their corruption and arrogance saddened him. One last time he reminded his people to obey Allah and treat all men with fairness and respect. One last time the Banu Israil listened to their prophet and were sorry and repented. As he left them to go back up the mountain he heard them weeping and promising to keep Allah's Law. Yusha ﷺ died peacefully at 110 in his retreat on the mountain and that is where he was buried.

May Allah bless Yusha ﷺ and give him peace.

Samuel ﷺ

And their Prophet said to them: surely Allah has raised Talut to be king over you. (2:246)

19

And the Light Passed to Samuel ﷷ

After Yusha ﷷ died Allah did not send another prophet for over eighty years. During this time the Banu Israil forgot their promise to Yusha ﷷ and their repentance. They fell away from the Law of the Torah and the teachings of their prophets. Allah punished them by making them suffer the attacks of their unbelieving neighbors.

The twelve tribes began to quarrel with each other. They had no leader to whom all would listen. Each one wanted to be the leader. Their greatest enemy, however, was a people whose king was called Goliath. Goliath was large and strong. He saw the disunity of the tribes of Israil and he took the opportunity to attack. Not only did he vanquish the small force that came out to meet him but he also managed to take the Ark among the spoils. The Banu Israil still carried with them the Ark of the Covenant that had been given to Seth ﷷ and they had placed in it the broken stones on which the Torah had been chiseled. They took it with them to war because it brought Allah's blessing.

In the year the Ark was taken a baby boy was born to Hannah ﷺ.

Hannah had been unable to have children. When she was quite old she delivered a baby boy who she named Samuel, meaning, "Allah has heard". The light of Muhammad shone on his forehead like the sun on a clear day. He was sent to the temple to study the law with the priests. When he was twenty-nine he was told that he had been chosen by Allah to be His prophet.

Samuel began to travel in the land talking to whoever would listen. He reminded them of their promises and of the Law and the one God Who created and loves them. Everywhere there was fear and despair: fear of the enemies who encircled them, despair that without the Ark or a leader they could never survive. The Banu Israil asked Samuel to find them someone to be their king, to recover the Ark and vanquish their enemies. Samuel was concerned that his people would repeat the past. Even with leaders and prophets they had still backed away from fighting. So he did what they wanted and asked Allah to appoint someone from among them to be their king.

One day a young man named Talut came to greet Samuel and ask for help in locating his lost camels. Talut was a large and handsome young man but his family was poor and undistinguished. Allah told Samuel that He had chosen Talut to be the king of Israil and one of the signs would be the return of the Ark. Talut was astounded. He was a poor shepherd, unlearned and unprepared. The Banu Israil were also unhappy. This was not the king they had expected, and they doubted his ability. But when they saw the Ark, carried by angels, arrive at Talut's small house they began to understand. Regardless of appearances or origins a man's true value lies in his heart. Allah had chosen Talut.

The Banu Israil rallied around Talut, and set out for battle with Goliath. As news of the size of the enemy army reached them they began to lose heart. Talut promised his daughter in marriage and the kingship to whoever would kill Goliath. Still men quietly slunk away and deserted. The army came to a river and Talut ordered the soldiers not to drink too much or they would become sick and be unable to fight. This was his first command and most of his men disobeyed. They drank and became unable to fight. Of the hundred thousand who had set out only four thousand now followed Talut into battle. Goliath waited for them with an army eighty thousand strong.

The courage of the Banu Israil failed. Goliath, the enemy king, was a giant of a man, huge and strong. He towered above them and challenged any man to single combat. No one stepped forward. Talut could find no champion among the Banu Israil. Samuel ﷺ made a special suit of armor. He gave this to Talut telling him that by Allah's command the man it fitted perfectly would be their champion. Talut ordered all the Banu Israil to try on this suit of armor. It fit none of them.

Among the soldiers were the eight sons of Jesse. They were brave and disappointed that the armor was too big for them. They had a young brother named Da'ud ﷺ who was only thirteen years old and small for his age. He had big beautiful eyes and a voice so sweet that the birds stopped to listen when he sang. His father would not let him fight so he only helped his brothers and carried their food. At home he protected the flocks of his father from lions and he had become very skilled with the slingshot. He had followed slowly behind the army. When he arrived he told his father of a strange experience. Three pebbles on the road had greeted him and insisted he pick them up. He had put them in his pocket. They were, actually, three pieces of the mountain that had disintegrated when Musa ﷺ asked to see Allah face to face.

Now Talut saw the latecomer and insisted he try on the suit of armor like everyone else. To their amazement the armor fit him perfectly although he was much smaller than the others for whom it had been too big. It was clear that Da'ud ﷺ had been chosen by Allah to fight the giant Goliath. But it was not clear that this would lead to victory. The Banu Israil prepared for defeat and the sons of Jesse mourned the certain death of their little brother.

Da'ud ﷺ stood and faced Goliath. He had removed the armor of Samuel ﷺ because it was uncomfortable. He held his slingshot in one hand and the three pebbles in the other. Goliath taunted him. "Oh child" he said, "Go back to your mother." But Da'ud ﷺ picked up his sling and aimed for Goliath's head. Allah directed the three pebbles to their mark on the forehead of Goliath. Goliath fell to the ground, dead. His army was terrified. They fled and were pursued by the Israilites who gained a great victory that day.

Samuel ﷺ, Da'ud ﷺ and Talut returned to the palace among crowds of people singing and rejoicing. But envy crept into Talut's heart because the people praised Da'ud ﷺ more than they praised him. Talut did not give his oldest daughter to Da'ud ﷺ in marriage as he had promised. Da'ud ﷺ lived in the palace making chain mail for the soldiers by hand in a new way that Allah had taught him. Talut's younger daughter loved Da'ud ﷺ and asked her father to marry her to him. Talut sent Da'ud ﷺ against the enemy army, without the Ark, hoping he would be killed. Da'ud ﷺ returned victorious, by Allah's Will, and Talut had no choice but to marry him to his daughter.

Now Shaytan had possession of Talut. Everywhere the king saw imaginary enemies especially in the loving heart of Da'ud ﷺ. Everyone admired Da'ud ﷺ more than Talut and Talut's jealousy knew no bounds. Samuel ﷺ counseled Talut one last time but to no avail. Then Samuel ﷺ returned to his home accompanied only by Da'ud ﷺ where he died and was buried. It seemed Israil was without a prophet.

May Allah bless Samuel ﷺ and give him peace.

Da'ud ﷺ

We (Allah) caused the hills and the birds to join Daud in celebrating Our praises. (21:74)

20

And the Light Passed to Da'ud ﷺ

The mind of Talut became more and more unstable until Da'ud ﷺ was forced to flee for his life into the wilderness. Talut gave Da'ud's ﷺ wife to another man in marriage. Da'ud ﷺ was no longer the king's son-in-law and the soldiers hunted for him as for an animal. Talut could not bear the critical looks of the priests and wise men. They saw the light on Da'ud ﷺ and the darkness on Talut. So Talut had all the priests and wise men put to death.

In the wilderness men of true faith gathered around Da'ud ﷺ. They formed a band of soldiers that patrolled the southern borders of the kingdom of Israil. Even though considered outlaws by the king they continued to help protect the kingdom.

Da'ud ﷺ had been given by Allah a special talent. He could put the Divine Love that filled his heart into words and music. He had such a beautiful voice that the wild animals would gather around him to listen and the people who heard him could not help but be moved to tears of joy.

For seven years Da'ud ﷺ and his men lived in caves hiding from the king. In this time Da'ud ﷺ married several wives and had many children.

Finally Talut regained some of his sense. He regretted his treatment of Da'ud ﷺ and realized how much he had disobeyed Allah. He wanted to repent and ask forgiveness but he did not know how. He had killed all the priests and wise men so there was no one left to teach him. He wept day and night. Finally a sympathetic guard told him of the existence of one wise old lady. She told Talut to dress for battle and go out to fight the enemy as a common foot soldier, he and most of his sons.

They did this and all of them were martyred in battle. Da'ud ﷺ mourned their deaths but believed that they had in this way achieved forgiveness. One son remained alive and he declared himself king and began to hunt Da'ud ﷺ as his father had before him. Da'ud ﷺ spent most of his nights in prayer. One night the angel Jibrail ﷺ appeared and filled the whole sky with light. He announced to Da'ud ﷺ his prophethood and gave him the first verses of a book that was to be called *Zaboor* (Psalms). All night Da'ud ﷺ conversed with the angel who taught him from the Wisdom of the Lord.

Now the Banu Israil flocked around Da'ud ﷺ. The light of Muhammad ﷺ shone ever brighter from his brow. Soldiers deserted the son of Talut who was finally killed by one of his own guards.

Now Da'ud ﷺ was king of all Israil and a prophet of Allah as well. He established Jerusalem as his capitol. He brought the Ark there, and began to build a mosque on the site of a great rock that miraculously hung in the air. His reign lasted forty years. During all this time the revelation of the *Zaboor* continued. It consisted of one hundred and fifty chapters and it was a book of song and praise of Allah.

Da'ud ﷺ took back his first wife, the daughter of Talut, and he also married many more women. They say he had ninety-nine wives and many children. Da'ud ﷺ, even when he was king, continued to make coats of mail with his own hands in order to support himself and his large family.

Allah Almighty declared that the kingship of Israil should remain in the family of Da'ud ﷺ. But Da'ud ﷺ had nineteen sons all of whose faces shone with the light of Muhammad ﷺ. He feared they might fight after his death unless one was chosen to follow him as king. Jibrail ﷺ told Da'ud ﷺ to have each of his sons plant their staff in sand that had been poured onto the floor of a closed room. The staff that became green and alive by morning would signal who should be the next king. The sons planted their dry sticks, each with his name carved upon it. In the morning the staff belonging to Sulayman ﷺ had grown as high as the ceiling and was sprouting with branches and green leaves. So it was known without doubt whom Allah had chosen to succeed Da'ud ﷺ.

Da'ud ﷺ lived for one hundred years and he left this world on a Saturday. He died while in prayer and was buried in his own city of Jerusalem.

May Allah bless Da'ud ﷺ and give him peace.

Luqman عليه السلام

And certainly We gave Luqman wisdom. (31:12)

21

And the Light Passed to Luqman ﷺ

Luqman ﷺ is mentioned in the Holy Qur'an as a wise man. Some say he was a prophet, others that he was a saint and friend of Allah.

He was born in Nubia in upper Egypt but he moved with his family to the area of Jerusalem in the time of Da'ud ﷺ. It was mentioned to Da'ud ﷺ that a stranger had arrived in the kingdom who was very wise and also very black. Da'ud ﷺ immediately went to welcome him, reminding the people that Allah had made their father Adam ﷺ of all colors of the earth. The color of a man's skin is of no importance to Allah, only the condition of his heart.

Luqman ﷺ was a keeper of eagles. He raised and fed them all the days of his life. He would raise one from a chick and when it was getting old he would use it to train a new chick. Then he would set the old one free. The life span of an eagle is eighty years. Luqman ﷺ counted his years by the years of his eagles. When he arrived in Israil he had already raised four eagles. He must have been about three hundred and twenty years old.

Luqman ﷺ saw immediately the light of Muhammad ﷺ upon the brow of Da'ud ﷺ and he knew Da'ud ﷺ would be a prophet before Da'ud ﷺ himself knew. Da'ud ﷺ asked Luqman ﷺ to remain in Israil to help him guide the people who were in constant danger of forgetting and going back on their promises. Luqman ﷺ became a teacher to the Banu Israil. He served Da'ud ﷺ before he became prophet and king and later Luqman ﷺ served him as an official advisor.

Luqman ﷺ had a small son to whom he gave advice of such timeless wisdom that Allah recorded it in His Book the Holy Qur'an. Allah added emphasis to Luqman's ﷺ words by telling all children the proper way to treat their parents. Allah said, "Be kind and respectful to your parents. Your mother delivered you with hard labor and cared for you when you were unable to care for yourself. So be thankful to your parents and to Allah. Obey your parents unless they demand you worship other than Allah. Keep them company in this life with kindness. Follow the path of those who turn towards Allah because He is the goal of your journey and in the end He will explain to you everything that you did not understand."

Luqman ﷺ told his son, "Oh my little son do not look for Divine Power from anyone but Allah alone. For to think there is someone with the power to help you other than God is a great mistake."

Luqman ﷺ continued, "Oh my dear son, whatever happens in this world no matter how small or seemingly insignificant, Allah knows about it. Nothing can be hidden from Him, not in the depths of the earth nor the heights of the skies. Allah is aware of all things. Establish regular prayers.

Advise people to do what is right and forbid the doing of wrong. Whatever difficulties you may face keep patient."

"My son", he said, "Do not look down on other people as if you were better than they are. Allah does not love those who are proud. Be modest and humble in your behavior and speak gently so that you do not resemble the braying donkey."

(This is a paraphrase of Qur'an, Surah Luqman: ayats 13-19.)

Luqman ﷺ raised three more eagles in his lifetime, making seven in all. He lived until the time of the prophet Yunus ﷺ and died at the age of five hundred and sixty years.

May Allah bless Luqman ﷺ and give him peace.

Sulayman ﷺ

Around Sulayman were gathered his companies of Jinn, men and birds. (27:17)

22

And the Light Passed to Sulayman ﷺ

When Da'ud ﷺ died the angel Jibrail ﷺ came to console Sulayman ﷺ. He asked him one question from his Lord: "Would you rather have the kingship or would you rather have knowledge?" It is said that three quarters of all the wisdom given to men was given to Sulayman ﷺ, and so he answered Jibrail ﷺ that he preferred knowledge from Allah to kingship over worldly things. Allah was pleased with his answer and for this reason gave Sulayman ﷺ both the kingdom and the knowledge.

Then, on Friday, the tenth of Muharram, Ashura, by order of Allah, Jibrail ﷺ gave Sulayman ﷺ the Ring of Power which shone like a star in the sky. This ring had belonged to Adam ﷺ in Paradise but when he left he had lost it.

Sulayman ﷺ wound the royal turban of his father Da'ud ﷺ around his head and took the staff of Musa ﷺ in his hand. He unfurled the flag of Yusuf ﷺ and put the ring of Adam ﷺ on his finger. Then he went out to his people in his full majesty, commander of the seen and the unseen, and by Allah's permission, the greatest sultan the world has known.

The wind blew at his command carrying him wherever he wished. The Jinn slaved at his orders bringing treasures out of the depths of the earth and the sea and fashioning them into beautiful things. The Jinn made him a carpet three miles square covered in beautiful patterns and magical symbols. Upon this carpet they placed Sulayman's ﷺ throne surrounded by two thousand seats for the holy men and seers he kept to advise him. Behind them was a row of twelve thousand seats for the priests and teachers. There were also seventy thousand places of prayer for the saints and dervishes who were always worshipping and doing dhikr. And the wind carried this carpet wherever Sultan Sulayman ﷺ wished to go.

On this carpet Sulayman ﷺ traveled to see the wondrous signs of Allah in the wide world. Everywhere he went he brought knowledge of Allah the One God, His Law and His Peace.

When Sulayman ﷺ was sultan the justice of his courts became legendary. Even as a child Sulayman ﷺ had been interested in the business of the sultan. He would sit in his father's court and listen carefully to all that went on there, and then would reenact with his playmates what he had seen. In his play Sulayman ﷺ would often make judgments that were wiser and more just than his father had made in the real court. Sometimes his father would hide near by and listen. Da'ud ﷺ was able in this way to take advice from his little son.

Sulayman ﷺ was also given the ability to understand the speech of all creatures. One day while traveling at the head of his army he heard a small ant warning his fellow ants to run or be trampled. The ant wondered why a king with so much would destroy a small ant colony with so little. Sulayman ﷺ in humility ordered his huge army to march in a wide circle around the ant and his colony.

Sulayman ﷺ took regular council with the birds. They would tell him the state of his kingdom as they saw it from the air. One day the sultan noticed the long absence of the hoopoe bird. When he returned the hoopoe told Sulayman ﷺ of a wondrous kingdom to the south. The ruler was a Queen who was both beautiful and wise but she and all her people worshipped the sun. Sulayman ﷺ immediately sent a letter to this Queen, whose name was Bilqis ؑ, inviting her to visit him and learn about Allah Almighty, her Creator. The hoopoe took the letter to her.

Bilqis ؑ was afraid Sulayman ﷺ would come with his army and destroy her people so she decided to send him a gift. She gathered together the best of all she had, bricks of gold and silver, pearls the size of ostrich eggs and jewels of untold value. When Sulayman ﷺ received this gift he sent it back to her with a letter. He wrote that what he had offered her, knowledge of Allah, was of far greater value than the material things that she offered him. The only gift he desired from her was for her to believe in Allah and he invited her again to visit his court.

Bilqis ؑ knew now that Sulayman ﷺ was no ordinary king. But she was proud and still thought that her way of understanding was correct. She gathered her entire army around her and traveled north.

Sulayman ﷺ had a special palace built to receive Bilqis ؑ. He ordered the Jinn to pave a twenty mile square with gold and silver tiles in intricate designs. Along all its sides he stationed the Jinn and *Ifrits*, dragons and monsters. In the center he placed his great throne. Next to it he placed the throne of Bilqis ﷺ or one exactly like it. Leading up to this magnificent court was a hall whose floor was made of clear crystal that looked like water.

When Bilqis ﷺ saw the hall of glass she became afraid because she thought it was magic. After some hesitation she overcame her fear, trusted her heart and lifted her skirts to wade in. Only then she found that her eyes had been fooled. Things are not always the way they appear. Her feet remained dry and she safely approached Sulayman's ﷺ throne. Then she saw in front of her a thing that could not be, her very own throne which she had left behind in her palace. Sulayman ﷺ asked her if this was in fact her throne. Since she had just learned that the eye is not always a good judge, she replied cautiously that it did indeed look like her throne.

Sulayman ﷺ understood from her reply that she was humbled and so he stepped out from behind the curtain of his throne and greeted her. Her heart now open, Bilqis ﷺ saw the light streaming from his face and accepted Allah as her Creator and Sulayman ﷺ as her prophet. Soon afterwards they were married.

Da'ud ﷺ had begun the building of the great mosque in Jerusalem but he had not been able to complete it. Now Sulayman ﷺ took over the task of his father. All the treasures at his command he poured into the making of this glorious place of worship. Day and night he kept the Jinn at work building and decorating. As his death approached he begged Allah to allow him to finish the mosque, because he knew that the Jinn would stop working as soon as he was gone. Allah caused Sulayman ﷺ to die while standing, leaning on his staff at a window overlooking the mosque. The Jinn thought he still lived and they continued work. Only on the day the mosque was completed did Allah allow the staff, eaten by worms, to crumble to dust. This was not the powerful staff of Musa ﷺ, which Allah removed from the world and keeps hidden.

At this time the people and Jinn realized Sulayman ﷺ had left them. No one knows where he was buried, but at his request whoever prays two *rakats* at the site of his mosque will be forgiven all their past mistakes.

May Allah bless Sulayman ﷺ and give him peace.

Iliyas ﷺ

And Zakariya and Yahya and Isa' and Iliyas: all of them are among the righteous. (6:86)

23

And the Light Passed to Iliyas ﷺ

After the death of Sulayman ﷺ his son, Rehoboam, became king. But he was not a prophet like his father, and the rebellious tribes of Israil refused to accept his authority. Ten of the tribes left and appointed their own king. Israil was split into two parts, North and South. In the north Rehoboam ruled with his capitol at Jerusalem, the site of the temple of Sulayman and the Ark of the Covenant. In the south they began to worship idols again and follow their every desire. North and South fought each other for 57 years, until Rehoboam's son, Jehoshaphat, ruled the North and Ahab ruled the South.

Out hunting one day, King Ahab encountered a man from whose forehead the light streamed like a beacon through the fog. Ahab asked his name. He answered he was Iliyas ﷺ, descendant of Harun ﷺ. Iliyas ﷺ and Ahab were the same age, young men of twenty-five. They became best friends. Iliyas ﷺ spoke earnestly about their ancestors, the prophets, and Allah. They prayed together and Ahab happily took counsel with Iiyas ﷺ. Ahab saw the light and became convinced. He determined to change himself and his kingdom.

Ahab made a treaty with Jehoshphat and the kingdom of Israil united in peace. People seemed to love Iliyas ﷺ and listened to his preaching. Things looked like they were getting better. But Shaytan was jealously waiting for his chance. He saw the weakness of Ahab. Shaytan caused Ahab to fall in love with an idol-worshipping princess. Her name was Jezebel and not only was she very beautiful but she was also very hardhearted and only loved herself. She did not just want to be Queen. She wanted to be worshipped. She told Ahab that she would marry him only if he built a huge statue in her image and encouraged all people to worship it.

Ahab was madly in love. He agreed to do as Jezebel requested. He was ashamed before his friend Iliyas ﷺ and for a while refused to see him. In the end he announced his plans to build idols for the Banu Israil. Iliyas ﷺ, seeing the uselessness of argument, left the palace and his friend.

Ahab told his people that he was building them a great god with the body of a cow and the face of a beautiful woman (Jezebel). He said the earth, the cow, and the woman should all be worshipped as symbols of the life-giving force. His people were delighted and the building began immediately. They named their idol, Baal.

Ahab married Jezebel. Jezebel asked the king to sacrifice those closest to him to the new god. Ahab was surprised to hear this from a fifteen-year-old girl but he did what she wanted. Then she found fault with the priests who still listened to Iliyas ﷺ. She had all four hundred of them killed. Her temple was awash with blood.

Iliyas ﷺ went from town to town preaching. Few listened and the others began to threaten him. He suffered great hardship. Finally he announced he was going to the hills to live by himself in a cave. Inspired by Allah, he told them that the Queen would give birth to a sickly son who would die because there was no life-giving force in her or her idol.

It happened as Iliyas ﷺ predicted. The baby son of Jezebel and Ahab became ill. Ahab, now completely under the spell of his Queen, sent soldiers to kill Iliyas ﷺ thinking he had cursed the baby. But Allah protected His prophet. So the Queen decided that to cure her son they needed to bathe Baal in blood. She ordered that all the children of Israil be killed so that her son could live. It was done. Still Jezebel's baby did not get well. Ahab knew that the only one with true power was Iliyas ﷺ because his power came from the Source of all life, Allah Almighty. But Iliyas ﷺ did not have Allah's permission to heal the baby and he died.

Iliyas ﷺ returned to preaching to the common people hoping they would end their worship of Baal. While he was among them, the idea of killing him or taking him captive did not even cross their minds. He warned them of Allah's Punishment. He told them that no rain would fall and no food would grow and hunger would torment them. But they did not believe. It happened as Iliyas ﷺ had warned. There was no rain. The animals died. The crops withered. The people starved. And still they continued to sacrifice and pray to the terrible Baal.

Iliyas ﷺ remained in the south wandering from village to village. Allah gave him the miraculous power to produce freshly baked bread at will. Whoever took him in ate fresh bread. People knew where Iliyas ﷺ had passed because the smell of freshly baked bread lingered in the air. Even with this miracle the people stubbornly refused to believe. Ahab instructed his soldiers that wherever they detected the smell of bread they should kill everyone. Then no one invited Iliyas ﷺ into their homes even though they were starving.

Allah ordered Iliyas ﷺ to leave Israil and go to a city by the sea. There he should look for an old widow. This women and her husband were descendants of Yusuf ﷺ. When they were in their nineties they were overwhelmed by the desire to have a child. They were the only believers left in the city. They didn't want the love of Allah to die out. So they prayed for a son and Allah granted their prayer. They named him Alyas'a ﷺ, meaning, "May it please God." After four years her husband died and now she was alone.

Iliyas ﷺ found the widow's house and seeing the light streaming from his brow she invited him in. He met Alyas'a ﷺ on the balcony doing what he loved best, watching the dolphins play in the sea.

For two months Iliyas ﷺ stayed at the widow's house. Then one day Alyas'a ﷺ became very ill. It appeared that he had died. Iliyas ﷺ prayed to Allah to save the boy and make him one of His special servants. Alyas'a ﷺ breathed and sat up.

Allah ordered Iliyas ﷺ to return to King Ahab. It had been four years since it had rained. Iliyas ﷺ and Ahab made an agreement. Ahab would pray to Baal for rain. If it came, Iliyas ﷺ would leave the land. If not, then Iliyas ﷺ would pray to Allah for rain. If it came, Ahab would destroy the idol. First

Ahab's priests prayed. Nothing happened. Then Iliyas ﷺ prayed. Allah sent rain and the country became green again and the wells filled with water. But Ahab did not keep his promise.

Now Iliyas ﷺ knew Allah's Punishment was coming and he warned Ahab and Jezebel and all the people. They ignored him and he left. He wept because he felt he had failed Allah and failed his people. Seventeen years went by during which they endured wars, invasions, heavy taxes, disease and natural disaster. Finally the people could take no more. Jezebel and Ahab were killed by an angry mob and their bodies thrown to the dogs. Allah told Iliyas ﷺ to find Alyas'a ﷺ. They retreated together to a cave in the hills where Iliyas ﷺ taught Alyas'a ﷺ everything he knew.

May Allah bless Iliyas ﷺ and give him peace.

Alyas'a ﷺ

And Ismail and Alyas'a and Yunus and Lut: and all of them we favored above the nations. (6:87)

24

And the Light Passed to Alyas'a ﷺ

Iliyas ﷺ was old and sad. He had suffered much at the hands of the very people he was sent to help. He knew his days on earth were numbered. Iliyas ﷺ prayed to Allah not to let him be killed by his own people. He did not wish the sin of his murder to be on their hands. He also prayed to be allowed to live until the time of the last prophet, the Prophet Muhammad ﷺ, so that he could greet him and be part of his community.

Then Iliyas ﷺ asked Alyas'a ﷺ what he could give him as a parting gift. Alyas'a ﷺ asked for a spiritual gift. He asked to continue in the footsteps of his beloved teacher Iliyas ﷺ. This made Iliyas ﷺ sad for he knew the heavy burden that his dearest follower would inherit. He gave Alyas'a ﷺ his cloak and his leather belt and kissed him good-bye.

Just then they saw far off in the sky a shape of fire descending towards them. As it got closer they could see it was a fiery horse. Jibrail ﷺ appeared and gave Iliyas ﷺ greetings of peace from Allah, Lord of the worlds. He told him his prayers were accepted. Iliyas ﷺ, without fear, climbed on the back of the horse of fire and was carried into the heavens where he lives to this day in the same way as the prophet Idris ﷺ.

Fear took hold of Alyas'a's ﷺ heart as he realized that he had asked for the heaviest burden there is and he prayed to Allah to forgive him. But Jibrail ﷺ came to strengthen his heart with news that Allah had chosen Alyas'a ﷺ to be His prophet. With that Alyas'a ﷺ forgot all the hardship he and Iliyas ﷺ had suffered. Alyas'a ﷺ put on the cloak and the belt of Iliyas ﷺ and the light of his prophethood, like the beacon of a lighthouse, shone out over the land all the way to the sea.

Most of the people in Israil were relieved at the disappearance of Iliyas ﷺ. They quickly forgot about him and paid no attention to his companions. The believers gathered around their prophet and began to live normal quiet lives.

Alyas'a ﷺ married and had a family. One of his sons carried the light brightly on his brow. His name was Yunus ﷺ. Alyas'a ﷺ took him once to the city by the sea to visit the grave of his grandmother. Together they watched the dolphins play as Alyas'a ﷺ had done as a child. The dolphins seemed particularly tame and friendly with Yunus ﷺ.

In the kingdom of Israil things were not going well. Now on both sides, North and South, the people worshipped idols. They forgot their Lord, His books and His prophets. There was no justice in the land. The rich grew richer and the poor grew poorer. The Anger of Allah was upon them. Drought, hunger, earthquakes and disease were everywhere. Allah gave Alyas'a ﷺ permission to perform amazing miracles because in such times nothing else will get the attention of the unbelieving and forgetful people. Alyas'a ﷺ took up his wanderings again in order to reach as many people as possible. Nothing he saw gave him much hope. To lead a life of virtue in Israil at that time was almost a forbidden thing.

Leprosy began to spread in the land. This is a terrible disease in which the body slowly decays and rots away while the person remains alive. There was no cure. Allah gave Alyas'a ﷺ the ability to heal leprosy. Wealthy and poor came to him to be healed and many of them listened to his words and became believers in the one God.

The believers were now so numerous that they lived everywhere in every town and village. They began to get caught up in the wars and affairs of the state of Israil. So Alyas'a ﷺ accompanied the armies in order to give protection to the believers who were there. He performed many miracles, saving the armies but the people in power did not change. The mosque in Jerusalem was filled with idols and filth. The majority of people persisted in their unbelief.

Alyas'a ﷺ was nearly eighty years old, when his beloved son Yunus ﷺ asked him for permission to travel in the land and seek his fortune. Alyas'a ﷺ told him to go to a large city by the sea, the Assyrian capitol of Nineveh. This was the very place where the young prophet Ibrahim ﷺ had smashed all the idols with his axe. But Yunus ﷺ was too shy to aspire to the station of Ibrahim ﷺ and asked only for the station of his axe. Alyas'a ﷺ wondered at this for he had asked for the prophethood himself before he really understood its burden. His son seemed shy to accept it even if it was his destiny.

Alyas'a ﷺ kissed his son farewell and Yunus ﷺ went out into the world.

They would never see each other again in this life for not long after Alyas'a ﷺ became ill. He talked to each of his followers and asked them to promise to protect their faith, remember Allah and keep the Law of Musa ﷺ. Each one promised and kissed his hand. Then quietly Alyas'a ﷺ left this world. He was buried where he died.

May Allah bless Alyas'a ﷺ and give him peace.

Yunus ﷺ

Then the big fish did swallow him. (37:142)

25

And the Light Passed to Yunus ﷺ

Yunus ﷺ left his father with sadness, knowing in his heart that they would not meet again in this world. He joined a caravan making its way to Nineveh. But Yunus ﷺ was pure and innocent. He was no match for the thieves that waited along the road. Soon he had lost all his property. He approached Nineveh with only a few coins in his pocket. Yunus ﷺ found himself in a town on the outskirts of the city, in which most of the people worked in clay. One man who spoke his language took him to an old man, potter to the king. This old man was looking for someone to whom to teach his craft. None of his own sons were interested. Yunus ﷺ apprenticed himself to this master potter.

After some time the old man became sick. He knew he was dying. He introduced Yunus ﷺ, now a skilled craftsman, to the king as his inheritor. The king liked Yunus ﷺ and, after checking him out, trusted him. He gave him a workshop near the palace and they became friends. Yunus ﷺ made beautiful things for the king, unlike anything they had ever seen before. In Nineveh all the objects were decorated with frightening, scowling faces of Jinn and monsters made to strike fear into the beholder. Yunus ﷺ made beautiful things full of the loveliness of nature. Yunus ﷺ learned the Assyrian language and settled down. He never spoke of religion because the Assyrians were idol worshippers and they had no patience for a God they could not see and touch.

After some time Yunus ﷺ heard of the death of his father and longed to return to visit his family. He asked permission of the king to make a visit home. The king reluctantly agreed. On the way Yunus' ﷺ caravan passed a village. Something warned Yunus ﷺ that all was not right with the village. Yunus ﷺ advised the members of the caravan not to enter the village. But they were hungry and they went anyway. Yunus ﷺ waited but not one of them returned. He went on his way alone. Very soon he met a battalion of soldiers on their way to that very village. Yunus ﷺ warned them that the plague, a sickness with no cure that kills its victims very quickly, was raging there. The soldiers thanked him. Yunus ﷺ asked them to greet the king for him and they continued in opposite directions.

That night Yunus ﷺ had a frightening dream. He saw his father Alyas'a ﷺ as he had never seen him in life. Alyas'a ﷺ was furious. He yelled at his son: "How can you leave Nineveh? You were sent there by Allah Almighty. It is His permission you need to have, not that of the king. And Allah does not give you permission. Go back immediately and practice more patience."

Yunus ﷺ turned around and headed back to Nineveh. Soon he saw a light in the sky coming towards him. It got bigger and bigger until he recognized the angel Jibrail ﷺ. He informed Yunus ﷺ that Allah had chosen him to be His prophet and that his people and his work lay in Nineveh.

On Yunus' ﷺ return he found himself a hero. All the people considered him to have prevented the plague from entering their country. Yunus ﷺ began to speak to them about Allah. The king thought Yunus ﷺ had become crazy from a touch of the plague. The people of Nineveh laughed at him but did not hurt him because he had saved the city. For twenty years Yunus ﷺ talked to the Assyrians about Allah, their Creator, the Master of the seen and the unseen worlds. Not one person in all of Nineveh believed. Yunus ﷺ often despaired but Jibrail ﷺ would come to encourage him. It was all in Allah's plan.

One day Jibrail ﷺ came and told Yunus ﷺ the end was near. He must go to the king and tell him that his city had forty days to believe or Allah would send destruction upon them. The king became angry and threatened Yunus ﷺ. But not one of the other people seemed to give Yunus ﷺ a second thought.

Forty days passed and on the morning of the fortieth day Yunus ﷺ could stand it no more. "I leave these people to their punishment," he shouted. He boarded a ship, leaving Nineveh for the open sea where he could watch the dolphins that he loved. The ship had just set sail when a wild storm arose that tossed the boat in every direction. A huge fish rose out of the sea as if to smash the tiny boat. Yunus ﷺ knew then that the storm had been sent to punish Nineveh but the fish had been sent for him. Once again Yunus ﷺ had left Nineveh without the permission of his Lord. He had lost patience with and compassion for his people. The sailors threw Yunus ﷺ into the sea and watched as the huge fish swallowed him whole. The boat went on safely and the storm continued towards Nineveh.

Now the fish was under orders from Allah to swallow Yunus ﷺ, but it was not allowed to eat him. Yunus ﷺ was told to make a retreat in the stomach of the fish. For forty days in the dark stomach of the fish, in the depths of a pitch black sea, under a sunless sky Yunus ﷺ prayed for forgiveness. He made this *dhikr*: "There is no god but You. Glory be to You alone! I am among those who are lost in darkness." (Qur'an 21:87) Finally Allah forgave him.

Meanwhile the storm cloud traveled towards Nineveh and a wondrous thing occurred. For twenty years Yunus ﷺ had planted seeds and in one moment they all sprouted. The king of Nineveh and his people saw the cloud and began to believe. They prayed to Allah to save them from destruction. But of course they did not know how to pray or what to say and Yunus ﷺ, their prophet, was nowhere to be found. The dark cloud passed over. The sun came out and nothing was destroyed except the idols smashed to pieces in the temples.

Yunus ﷺ completed his forty days of retreat in the stomach of the fish and then he was spit out on the shore, naked and cold. His skin was wrinkled and soft from being wet for so long and the bright sun burned him. So Allah caused a vine to grow with large leaves to cover Yunus ﷺ and to shade him. A shepherd living nearby gave him food and water and told him that Nineveh had not been destroyed. Yunus ﷺ was angry at the news. So Allah caused the vine to wither and die. Yunus ﷺ cried at the loss of his vine. Then Allah scolded him for caring more about the vine than about a city full of Allah's finest creations, men. Yunus ﷺ again asked forgiveness from his Lord.

With the help of the shepherd who became his trusted servant, Yunus ﷺ made his way back to Nineveh. There he found the king and the people completely open to all his teaching. He taught them to pray and he taught them the Law. They built mosques where the idols had been, and they worshipped the one God Who created them and forgave them.

Yunus ﷺ married and had children. He is one of only two prophets who had the satisfaction of seeing the people to whom he was sent actually change and become believers. The prophet Muhammad ﷺ was the other one. Yunus ﷺ died and was buried where he had lived.

It may seem strange that Yunus ﷺ, although he was a prophet, acted several times in a way that displeased his Lord. It is said that all the prophets, by Allah's Will, made at least one mistake in their life except the last prophet, Muhammad Mustapha ﷺ, who was created to be the only complete and perfect man

May Allah bless Yunus ﷺ and give him peace.

Sha'ya ﷺ

Whenever a messenger came to you with what you did not like you were arrogant. Some you called liars and others you killed. (2:87)

26

And the Light Passed to Sha'ya ﷻ

After the death of Alyas'a ﷻ the Banu Israil grew even more forgetful of their history, their Lord and His commandments. But one day a just and God-fearing king appeared in Israil. His name was Hezekiah and Allah sent to him a prophet named Sha'ya ﷻ to be his strength and his support. With the light shining from Sha'ya's ﷻ brow they defended Jerusalem, the Temple, the Torah and the Ark against the dark forces trying to destroy them from within and without.

Hezekiah defended the Banu Israil with his armies and his justice. Sha'ya ﷻ defended it with the Words of Allah and wise counsel. When it appeared that Hezekiah was dying, Sha'ya ﷻ prayed to the Lord and Hezekiah was granted fifteen more years. There was peace in the land and belief entered the hearts of the people once more.

Sha'ya ﷻ went around the country giving talks in every town and village, mansion and hut. Allah Almighty spoke directly through him. Sha'ya ﷻ tried to show them that the world is like a ruined building. It has nothing to offer. Allah, however, is the Builder. He can raise it up or tear it down as He Wills. If you turn to Him, then whatever you wish becomes possible. It is

Allah who causes the rain to fall, the rivers to run, the trees to grow and the fruit to ripen. The wise man turns only to Allah and asks only from Allah.

Reality is the reverse of what it appears. Allah told Sha'ya ﷺ to tell the people that what looks good to them is of no value to Allah. The rich, the powerful, the famous, to Allah, are poor. But the poor, the humble, the weak are in Allah's eyes rich and worthy.

Then Allah inspired Sha'ya ﷺ with knowledge of the future. He warned about the destruction of the city of Jerusalem and the Temple. He told how the believers would be made slaves then they would regain their freedom and rebuild the temple. Sha'ya ﷺ told them that in the last days Allah would send a prophet who would neither read nor write but would speak only the Truth. This prophet would be kind and generous and would be known for his compassion. He would be a just king and a great prophet and would bring a new Book from his Lord. His name would be Ahmad (Muhammad) ﷺ and he would unite the whole world under one religion. His nation would be better than any before, and after him there would be no more prophets until the end of time.

When the Banu Israil heard these words they became very angry. Who was this nation other than their own, they wondered? They decided to kill their prophet because he had begun to tell them things they did not want to hear. Sha'ya ﷺ ran into the wilderness chased by the people, who a little while earlier had loved him and who now so easily turned from belief to unbelief. As they were closing in on him Allah caused a tree to split open and Sha'ya ﷺ stepped inside. The bark closed around him and he would have been safe, but Shaytan, who was invisibly leading the people in pursuit, grabbed the tail end of his robe. When the angry mob arrived they saw a piece of Sha'ya's ﷺ robe sticking out of the tree.

They took their axes and chopped the tree to pieces. Sha'ya ﷺ, within the trunk, died a martyr under their savage blows.

May Allay bless Sha'ya ﷺ and give him peace.

Armiya ﷺ

And there never was a people who did not have among them a person to warn them. (35:24)

27

And the Light Passed to Armiya ﷺ

At the death of Sha'ya ﷺ the angel came to Armiya ﷺ to announce to him that he had been chosen by Allah to be His prophet. The light shone bravely on the brow of Armiya ﷺ like the lantern on a ship which has begun to drift in the fog.

The Lord ordered Armiya ﷺ to preach to the people. He had never done anything like that before and he had no talent for speaking. He did not know what to say. But he obeyed anyway and Allah filled his heart with inspiration and his mouth with strong words. He warned the Banu Israil that they had killed their prophet Sha'ya ﷺ. If they did not ask for forgiveness and change their ways terrible things would happen to them. They would be invaded by an army of a cruel enemy, their cities destroyed, their Temple burned to the ground, and they would be taken captive and sold as slaves.

The Banu Israil did not listen. Just as they had gotten angry with Sha'ya ﷺ for speaking a truth they did not want to hear, so now they became furious at the words of Armiya ﷺ. They had him locked away in a prison.

It was not long before everything Armiya ﷺ had warned them about came to pass. The king of Babylon invaded Israil with a gigantic army and killed many people and laid waste to Jerusalem. The Temple was destroyed. The people were led off into slavery and cried many bitter tears.

Armiya ﷺ survived to console his people in captivity and to remind them of the Words of their Lord and to inspire them with hope for a better future if they repented.

May Allah bless Armiya ﷺ and give him peace.

Daniel ﷺ

Ibrahim and Ismail prayed...our Lord raise up from among them (our descendants) a messenger to recite to them Your signs, and teach them the book and wisdom and purify them. (2:129)

28

And the Light Passed to Daniel ﷺ

Among those led into slavery in Babylon were the young princes of the royal house of Israil. They were singled out to be educated and trained especially for the service of the King. One of these youths was Daniel ﷺ. From his brow shone a light like a guiding star, steady and true in the blackness of the darkest night.

One night the king of Babylon had a terrible nightmare. In the morning he could remember nothing of the dream except his overwhelming fear. He questioned all his wise men but they could tell him nothing. He threatened to kill all the learned men in the whole country if no one could tell him what he had dreamed.

Daniel ﷺ heard this news and, in order to save all those innocent lives, he prayed to Allah to reveal to him the mysterious dream. Then Daniel ﷺ went before the king and told him, "You have seen a strange sight indeed. You saw a monster. Its head was of gold, its chest of silver, its legs of copper, its feet of iron and its toes of clay. Suddenly you saw a stone fall from heaven and break this monstrous thing into a million pieces that all blew away. Then that stone from heaven began to grow until it became as big as a mountain."

The king immediately recognized his dream and he asked Daniel ﷺ to tell him its meaning. Daniel ﷺ told the king that the dream concerned the future. The condition of men and their rulers will become worse and worse over time, just as silver is less than gold and copper less than silver, until a time will come when only iron and clay will rule and that will be the lowest point. Then Allah Almighty will sweep away those kings and their kingdoms and establish His Own rule over the earth.

The king of Babylon was very impressed and he rewarded Daniel ﷺ with wealth and high position. Daniel ﷺ stayed at the court of the king of Babylon although he was free to go and in this way he helped many people and did much good.

All his days Daniel ﷺ was a man of God and he never departed from the way of Truth.

May Allah bless Daniel ﷺ and give him peace.

Uzair ﷺ

He (Allah) gives life to the dead and He is possessor of power over all things. (42:9)

29

And the Light Passed to Uzair ﷺ

After the exile in Babylonia came to an end the Banu Israil returned to Jerusalem and saw it had been totally destroyed. Uzair ﷺ, the prophet, sat by the remains of the Temple crying both day and night. He cried because in the ashes of the temple lay the Holy Books of the past, the Books of all the Prophets who had come before him. Not one single page still existed in all this world. He cried at the thought of what this loss would mean to the children yet to be born.

Uzair ﷺ looked about him at the destruction, the blackened fields where orchards had been, ashes where the Prophets had stood and prayed. The Temple of Sulayman ﷺ was gone, its treasures stolen. Uzair ﷺ, exhausted, lost hope that things could ever be put right again. He sat under a tree and tied his little donkey nearby. While he was absorbed this way the Lord of the Worlds sent the Angel of Death ﷺ to take his soul.

After some time Uzair ﷺ was wakened by a voice asking him how long he thought he had been asleep. Uzair ﷺ blinked in the sunlight and guessed maybe a day or so. The voice answered that Uzair ﷺ had been as if asleep for a full hundred years. Uzair ﷺ sat up quickly and looked about him. All he saw was a pile of bleached bones where his donkey should have been.

Again Uzair ﷺ heard the heavenly voice. This time it spoke to the pile of bones commanding them to join together into their former shape. Uzair ﷺ watched in wonder as the bones moved together and slowly flesh and nerves grew up around them. Finally skin spread over them until his little donkey was complete again. It shook itself and rose to its feet, alive.

The Lord then poured all the Holy Books into the heart of Uzair ﷺ. Taking pen and paper Uzair ﷺ wrote down all the Torah from memory without a single mistake, and he rejoiced. Allah made Uzair ﷺ His prophet for those times. Uzair ﷺ then boldly questioned his Lord as to the nature of Destiny or Fate in which we must all believe. "Why," he asked his Lord, "do You punish those who do evil when You made it their destiny to do evil things?" Allah answered Uzair ﷺ that it was not written for him to understand such things. Uzair ﷺ must be patient until he meets face to face with his Maker and all things become clear. He must never ask again for knowledge that is not his to know or Allah would erase his name from the Book of Prophets.

Uzair ﷺ then stood up and looked about him. The land was green and trees were growing tall. The Temple had been rebuilt. There were small villages dotting the hillside. He went quickly to the place he had left his family. An old, old women answered the door. "Do your remember Uzair the prophet," Uzair ﷺ asked her. "Yes," she said. "Please pray for my eyesight to be returned so I can see if it is really you." Uzair ﷺ prayed and the old woman could see again. She immediately recognized Uzair ﷺ because he had not changed at all in the hundred years. She called the whole village and told them of the miracle. Uzair ﷺ had a son who was still alive at one hundred and twenty years. He and Uzair ﷺ hugged each other for a long time and gave thanks to Allah. This was the first time that there was a father who was younger than his son.

Uzair ﷺ went about in the land preaching and teaching. Wherever he went he took his little donkey.

The donkey of Uzair ﷺ is one of the ten animals (that we know of) honored by Allah with eternal life in the highest Heaven. The other animals are: the dog named Qitmeer of the seven sleepers in the cave (Surat al-Kahf), the fish of Yunus ﷺ, the sheep sent to replace the sacrifice of Ismail ﷺ, the she camel of Salih ﷺ, the ant who protected his family from the army of Sulayman ﷺ, the hoopoe bird who counseled Sulayman ﷺ, the cow mentioned in Surat al-Baqara, the elephant who saved the Ka'aba in the year of the Prophet Mohammad's ﷺ birth (Surat al-Fil), and the camel named Qaswa of Sayyidina Muhammad ﷺ.

May Allah Bless Uzair ﷺ and give him Peace.

Dhul-Qarnain ﷺ

Truly We gave him power in the earth and the means for all things. (18:84)

30

And the Light Passed to Dhul-Qarnain ﵇

Dhul-Qarnain ﵇ is the title given to this Prophet in the Holy Qur'an. It means, "The possessor of the two horns." Most Muslims believe that it refers to Alexander the Great (known as Iskander in Arabic). However, as with Luqman ﵇, people disagree as to whether Dhul-Qarnain ﵇ was a prophet or not. Only Allah knows for sure.

Some say Alexander ﵇ was called Dhul-Qarnain ﵇ because he wore a helmet with two horns on it. Others say it is because he ruled the known world from east to west: east is one horn, west the second. Others understand that he was given possession of two worlds, the spiritual and the material worlds. Alexander Dhul-Qarnain ﵇ was both prophet and king, saint and soldier. The last prophet, Muhammad ﷺ would also be given possession of both a spiritual and an earthly kingdom. Allah described Muhammad's ﷺ station as two lengths of an archer's bow from the heavenly throne: each end of the bow is called a horn.

Alexander ﵇ was born to king Phillip of Macedonia. His father loved him very much and had him surrounded by the greatest teachers and scholars of his time. Aristotle was his main tutor. When he was twenty his father was killed and Alexander ﷺ inherited the throne. The first thing he did was to collect a great army and unite the warring states of his homeland, Macedonia. Sometimes force is needed to make peace. Then he moved east and united all of Turkey.

He had a large army but in most places he had no need to fight. The people welcomed him because he ruled with a light hand. He put the original rulers back in place if they were good. He taxed in reasonable amounts and he left the nations to rule themselves. Therefore the wise welcomed him while only the tyrants fought him and by Allah's Will, they were defeated.

The people of Egypt heard of Alexander ﷺ and they asked him to save them from an invasion of cannibals. By using cleverness he frightened the cannibals and saved Egypt. It became part of his empire.

Then Alexander ﷺ went east to face the king of the largest empire of that time, Darius king of Persia. He tried to convince Darius to surrender peacefully. Against the advice of his closest counselors, Darius decided to fight. He was defeated in many battles until he had to flee from his homeland. Darius was then killed by his own officers who hoped for a reward from Alexander ﷺ. But Alexander ﷺ detested treachery and punished the officers instead. He buried Darius as befits a king. Alexander ﷺ married Darius's daughter and left her family in charge. Then he traveled on.

Alexander Dhul-Qarnain ﷺ traveled with a large court of wise men and seers, saints and philosophers. He always consulted with them before he did anything. And in every new country he sought out their wise men to learn from them and take advice. He believed in Allah, the one God, and spent his nights in prayer and contemplation. His one desire was to see everything of interest in the whole wide world and learn the wisdom it had to offer. He stayed at most a few months in each place before moving on to a new adventure. In this way he traveled the known world from Greece all the way to China. The prophet Muhammad ﷺ was to say later, "Seek knowledge, even if it be in China." That is just what Alexander Dhul-Qarnain ؑ did.

As a result of his curiosity and search for wisdom he united the world from east to west in peace and prosperity. Under Alexander Dhul-Qarnain ؑ people were free to travel, free to exchange goods and ideas. He was one of the greatest emperors the world has ever known, and he had so many exciting adventures that only a few can be mentioned here.

In his travels he met people who lived to be one thousand years old. He met people who lived in the snow with no clothing or shelter. He met the queen of a country of women. He went to lands where the sun never rose. He saw lakes of mercury and plains of silver. He saw valleys where diamonds littered the ground like fallen leaves.

At one point he came to a city at the foot of a mountain. The people there begged him to save them from two tribes named *Yajooj* and *Majooj* who lived on the other side of the mountain. One of the tribes was small like dwarves and the other tall like giants. They were both very strong with pointed teeth like pigs. Their ears were so large that they rolled one up to use as a pillow and pulled the other over them as a blanket. They were covered with hair from head to toe and they were always hungry. When they attacked they ate everything in sight.

Alexander ﷺ ordered the people to fill the pass over the mountain with any object of metal they could find. Then a great fire was lit that heated the metal until it melted together and formed a dam of iron that could neither be broken nor climbed. This dam has imprisoned *Yajooj* and *Majooj* until the end of time. In the last days *Yajooj* and *Majooj* will break through, with Allah's permission, and devastate the earth. They will drink all the lakes and rivers dry and eat everything in sight for three years. Then Allah will destroy them and throw their bodies into the sea.

Dhul-Qarnain ﷺ moved on. He came to the banks of a black sea. He was told that at the other end of that sea was a spring. Whoever drinks from that spring will live forever. Alexander ﷺ took with him only two companions, one was Khidr ﷺ the teacher of Musa ﷺ and the other was the prophet Iliyas ﷺ. At one point they separated. Khidr ﷺ and Iliyas ﷺ found the spring and drank. But by Allah's decree, Alexander ﷺ did not find it. Khidr ﷺ received the ability to become invisible from that time on but he still serves Allah in this world and acts as a teacher and guide to the ones Allah has chosen. Khidr ﷺ protects those on land and Iliyas ﷺ watches over those on the sea.

Still Dhul-Qarnain ﷺ traveled on by horse and by boat until he could go no further. He turned around and on his way home he died. He was only thirty-three years old. On his deathbed he was asked which he loved more, his father or his teacher. Alexander Dhul-Qarnain ﷺ answered, "I love my teacher better. My father is the cause of my coming with a high position into this world, but my teacher is the cause of my leaving it for a much higher position in the next life."

Dhul-Qarnain ﷺ asked that he be put into his coffin with both hands visible on top, one hand holding a golden ball and the other open and empty. He asked that they carry his coffin the full length of his empire so that all the people could see and learn that even the Great Alexander ﷺ who had held the world in his hand, left the world empty-handed.

May Allah bless Dhul-Qarnain ﷺ and give him peace.

Zakaria ﷷ

Whenever Zakaria entered her place of prayer (mihrab) he found food with her. (3:36)

31

And the Light Passed to Zakaria ﷺ

After the Temple in Jerusalem was rebuilt there was peace in Israil for a while. At that time it was the custom for believing people to dedicate one of their sons to the Temple to be raised by the priests. At about five years old a boy would be sent to the Temple to live and be trained. In this way he would grow up pure, knowing nothing of the world or the darkness of sin. He would marry and continue to serve the Temple for the rest of his life.

Zakaria ﷺ was among the priests at this time serving the Temple. He was descended from Sulayman ﷺ and was already quite an elderly man when the angel informed him that Allah had chosen him to be His Prophet. He and his cousin Imran had married sisters. Hannah ﷺ was the wife of Imran ﷺ and she had many children. Elizabeth ﷺ was the wife of Zakaria ﷺ and she had never had any children. When Hannah ﷺ found herself pregnant again she decided that if it were a son she would dedicate him to the Temple. But she had a baby girl. Allah told Zakaria ﷺ to tell Hannah ﷺ that this girl was very special. She should be named Maryam ﷺ and although it had never been done before, she should be dedicated to the Temple.

Hannah did as the Lord instructed. Zakaria, Maryam's uncle, became her teacher and guardian. He guarded her carefully and watched over her with a fatherly eye until she reached the age of marriage. One cold winter day Zakaria came to her room and found her eating from a bowl of summer fruits, fresh figs and grapes. There was no earthly way for her to have gotten these fruits. Zakaria believed her when she told him that Allah had sent the fruit to her. After several day of witnessing this miracle, Zakaria became inspired. If Allah could send fresh figs in the winter to Maryam than maybe He could still send a son to a man in the winter of his life.

Zakaria went home and began praying. He asked Allah for a worthy son who would inherit from him the prophethood. Jibrail came to Zakaria to tell him that his prayer had been accepted. He and Elizabeth would have a son. They were told to name him Yahya, meaning, "He lives," and this son would be pure and especially blessed by Allah.

Nine months later, to the amazement of the people, Elizabeth, already an old woman, safely delivered a strong baby boy. They saw the light streaming from his forehead like the morning star signaling the dawn. They raised him with great care and love. Allah gave him wisdom while he was still a young boy. He was God-fearing and loving and obedient to his parents. Allah said about him: "Peace be upon Yahya the day he was born, and the day he dies and the day he is raised up alive." (Qur'an 19:15)

Zakaria lived long enough to see Yahya grow to manhood and to witness his being informed by the angel that Allah had chosen him to be His prophet.

May Allah bless Zakaria ﷺ and give him peace

Yahya ﷺ

And We granted him wisdom as a child, and kind-heartedness from Us and purity. (19:12-13)

32

And the Light Passed to Yahya ﷺ

Yahya ﷺ was a very serious little boy. He did not play with the other children but rather sought the company of holy men in the desert. He prayed and he cried constantly. He was always thinking of the Greatness of Allah and his own imperfections. So much did he cry that his cheeks were permanently marked by tears.

Zakaria ﷺ tried never to speak about Hellfire or punishment when Yahya ﷺ was around. But one day when Zakaria ﷺ thought Yahya ﷺ was absent he gave a talk in the Temple about the punishments of Hell. Yahya ﷺ heard and afterwards he ran sobbing wildly into the mountains. His parents searched for him for days. When they found him he was cold and wet and hungry, but he did not want to return home. He wanted to be left to pray and fast and beg his Lord for forgiveness. Only because he was obedient to his parents did he return home with them. They made him eat and put him to sleep in a warm bed. Yahya ﷺ slept straight through the morning prayer for the first time in his life. He awoke and saw it was already light and was horrified. He wept so bitterly that all the angels in all the seven heavens wept with him. Even Shaytan felt sorry that he had not awakened Yahya ﷺ, although in general it is Shaytan's greatest pleasure to watch people sleep through the morning prayer.

Yahya ﷺ cried so long and so sincerely that Allah finally promised him that he would never enter the fires of Hell. Only then did Yahya's ﷺ heart fill with joy and hope. After this he prayed in order to be allowed to experience the Beauty and Gentleness of his Lord and he thanked Him all the days of his life.

Yahya's ﷺ mission was to announce the coming of the last prophet and to bear witness to the next prophet, his cousin 'Isa ﷺ, and to be his helper. He never married or had a family. He wandered the land teaching and warning the people. He never feared anything but God Almighty. He always spoke the plain truth and so other people sometimes feared him. Those who do unjust or unkind things do not like being told about it. Eventually he offended the king of Jerusalem who had his soldiers cut the throat of Yahya ﷺ and bring his head to court on a platter.

Because of the terrible nature of his death it is said that at the end of time Yahya ﷺ will be given a knife and ordered by Allah Almighty to slit the throat of Death itself. After that time there will be no more death.

May Allah bless Yahya ﷺ and give him peace.

'Isa ﷺ

'Isa son of Maryam said: Oh Allah, our Lord, send down to us a table (of food) from heaven. (5:114)

33

And the Light Passed to 'Isa ﷺ

Zakaria ﷺ taught Maryam ﷺ in the Temple and he kept her secluded from the other children because she was the only girl. When he saw that the Lord spoke to her he knew that she had learned well. She depended entirely on Allah and was firm in the knowledge that all things come only through Allah, directly or indirectly. He is the only Source.

One day Maryam ﷺ looked up to see a strange man in her room. She became very frightened. He told her that he was the archangel Jibrail ﷺ come to announce that Allah had chosen her above other women. She would give birth to a baby who would be a great prophet. Maryam ﷺ was surprised. She wondered how this was possible since she was not yet married and did not even know any men except her old uncle. But Jibrail ﷺ reminded her that Allah had made Adam ﷺ without either mother or father. Her baby would be only without a father. He would be known as 'Isa ﷺ, the Messiah, son of Maryam ﷺ. She fell to the ground in thankfulness before Allah.

For nine months Maryam ﷺ carried her baby and all the time she could hear him inside her praising God. When her time came to deliver she left the village. She labored alone leaning on the trunk of a dead palm tree for support. She cried out in her pain and a voice consoled her. Allah sent a cool stream to run beside her and the dead palm became green and bent down to give her its dates. She washed the baby in the stream and carried him back to her people. Allah told her to remain silent and let the baby speak for her.

When she approached the village with the baby the priests and the people were horrified. What had she done? They began to think terrible thoughts about her because she had given birth to a child even though she was not married. She remained silent, only pointing to the baby. Baby 'Isa ﷺ in her arms addressed the doubts of the people. He said: "I am the servant of God, Who has given me His Book and made me His prophet. Blessed am I wherever I may be. He has made me to pray and give charity as long as I live and to hold my mother dear. He has not made me proud or unsuccessful. Peace be upon me the day I was born, the day I die and the day I am raised up alive." (Qur'an 19:31-34) From his forehead a light shone like the sun rising above the horizon.

For a while this satisfied the priests, but before long they forgot the miracles and rejected what they had heard and seen. They accused Zakaria ﷺ of being a corrupt guardian of Maryam ﷺ and forced him to flee for his life. Only one man who served the Temple with Zakaria ﷺ and Maryam ﷺ held firmly to what he had seen. He believed in the miracles of Allah. His name was Yusuf ﷺ and he took Maryam ﷺ in marriage in order to protect her and her blessed child.

The king of Jerusalem also heard of the miracle birth of 'Isa ﷺ and became afraid that 'Isa ﷺ was destined to replace him as king. So he decided to kill all young boys born at that time. Maryam ﷻ and Yusuf ﷺ fled to Egypt where they lived in safety for twelve years.

They returned to Jerusalem and 'Isa ﷺ took up his studies again at the Temple. In addition he taught the *Injil* which was the name of the Book that Allah had given to him before he was born. Yahya ﷺ studied with him and was the first to accept him as a prophet. Whereas Yahya ﷺ was always sad and lived in fear of the fires of Hell, 'Isa ﷺ was always joyful and lived in the hope of Paradise.

Allah gave 'Isa ﷺ the ability to perform many miracles. When he was still quite young he and his companions were playing with clay. His playmates challenged him to make his creation live. 'Isa ﷺ molded a little misshapen bird and blew on it. With Allah's permission the little bird flew off. That is the origin of the bat, an unlikely creature that looks as if it were made by a child.

'Isa ﷺ could heal the blind and cure the leper. He could bring the dead back to life. But the priests and scholars in authority disliked two things that he did. They were displeased when they learned that he had brought a new Book, which changed the Law to make it a little easier for the average person to follow. And they disliked it when he announced the coming of another prophet after him named Ahmad (Muhammad) ﷺ. The priests could not accept these things and they forced 'Isa ﷺ to leave the Temple.

Twelve men, however, did accept and dedicated their lives to serving and helping 'Isa ﷺ in his mission. They are known as the Hawariyun (those who whiten what has turned dark). They followed 'Isa ﷺ as he went from town to town teaching.

At one town the people asked that 'Isa ﷺ bring down from Heaven a table heavy with food. 'Isa ﷺ warned them that demanding miracles has consequences: those who still do not believe after witnessing the miracle must be punished. Still the people asked for the table. 'Isa ﷺ prayed to Allah to grant their wish. Soon they saw something surrounded by clouds descending from the sky. It was indeed a table. On it was fried fish, and loaves of bread, salad, butter, honey, olives, cream and small plates of salt. The people came to eat, first one group and then another, until the whole crowd had eaten from this small table. There was still more food. For three days people came and ate and the amount of food never became less. All who ate went away healthier or wiser or richer in some way.

After three days the table went back into the heavens. Many people believed after this. Those who did not believe, however, were turned into pigs and monkeys and went snorting and scampering into the hills. They were never heard of again.

'Isa ﷺ had long hair and reddish white skin. He was clothed in a rough wool robe and went barefoot. He wore no gold or silver and ate very little. He was gentle and kind. He had no interest whatsoever in the things of this world.

After many years the corrupt priests and the people in power became worried that there would be an uprising against them. They determined to get rid of the source of the trouble, the prophet 'Isa ﷺ. So they raided the place where he was staying and took prisoner a man who resembled him. But Allah had sent the angel Jibrail ﷺ to take 'Isa ﷺ safely to live in heaven. The courts condemned the man to die and they killed him. Everyone, even his mother Maryam ﷺ, believed it was 'Isa ﷺ who had died. They wept and they mourned. After eight days Allah permitted 'Isa ﷺ to return briefly to let them know that he was safe with Allah and had not died. He instructed them to go about the land and tell his story and teach the *Injil*.

At the end of time 'Isa ﷺ will return. He will descend from Heaven, supported on all sides by angels, onto the white minaret in Damascus. He will lead the forces of Good against the forces of Evil and he will be victorious. 'Isa ﷺ will then rule the world for forty years of peace and joy. He will live in Medina and when he dies he will be buried next to the prophet Muhammad ﷺ.

May Allah bless 'Isa ﷺ and his mother Maryam ﷺ and give them peace.

Muhammad ﷺ

Glory be to Him who carried His servant by night from the sacred mosque to the farthest mosque...that We might show him of Our signs. (17:1)

34

And the Light Returned to Muhammad ﷺ

In Arabia, in the stony valley of Mecca, near the place where Ismail's ؑ baby heel had kicked up the dirt and Zamzam flowed, near the place where Ibrahim ؑ had built the House of God, near the graves of so many of the other prophets, on a warm desert night in the year 570 CE, a baby was born. He was born to two pure descendants of Ibrahim ؑ through his son Ismail ؑ. Their names were Aminah ؓ and Abdullah ؓ. Abdullah ؓ did not live to see the birth of his only child. When Aminah ؓ gave birth she said the light was so bright that it lit up the dawn and the baby's face appeared like the radiant moon when it is full. This was the promised child, the one for whom the light had originally been created, the one to whom the light was returning. This was Muhammad ﷺ. All of creation rejoiced. The stones of the Ka'aba trembled with joy and the scent of heavenly perfume drifted through the narrow streets of Mecca.

Muhammad ﷺ was the first created and the last to appear. In him human nature was completed. He was the perfect man. Allah Almighty created all of the rest of the world from the light of Muhammad ﷺ and created Muhammad ﷺ to be the light and the mercy for that world. Throughout his life Muhammad ﷺ prayed constantly for the forgiveness and welfare of all of creation and after his death his prayer continues.

Allah Almighty, however, did not give this beloved child a painless life in this world. His father had died before he was born. His mother died when he was six. He went to live with his grandfather, Abdul Muttalib ﷺ, who died only a few years later. Muhammad ﷺ was triply orphaned by the age of eight. He went to live in the big family of his father's brother, Abu Talib ﷺ. He was the poor son of a wealthy family. He was loved and cared for but he would have to find his own place in a world that had little compassion for the weak or helpless.

Muhammad ﷺ began to train as a merchant. He traveled with a caravan taking goods in trade to Damascus. Bahira ﷺ, the wise Christian monk, in his cave in the desert saw the cloud of Mercy following the caravan and recognized the light in the face of the young camel boy. He saw the seal of prophecy, a mark on Muhammad's ﷺ back, and he knew for certain that the one foretold, Ahmad ﷺ, had come.

Most of the people in Mecca were not learned and clear-sighted like Bahira ﷺ. But they saw something special in this young orphan boy. They trusted him with their belongings and their lives. He could be relied on. He could be believed.

When it came time to rebuild the Ka'aba, which had fallen into disrepair, the people of Mecca came to Muhammad ﷺ to resolve their differences. Together they built the walls, but it was by Muhammad's ﷺ blessed hand that the Black Stone was placed back in its corner.

A beautiful widow, Khadija ﷺ, noticed him and was impressed with his qualities. They married. She gave him six children, two boys who died in infancy and four girls, Zainab ﷺ, Umm Kulthum ﷺ, Ruqayya ﷺ, and Fatima ﷺ. Muhammad ﷺ did well for an orphan in that society. He was a loving husband and father. He was a successful merchant and a participant in the politics of his country. But in his heart he remained always in the company of Allah. He was in a constant state of spiritual vision, although outwardly he appeared like everyone else. But not all of creation was as blind as the people. The stars, the wind, the animals and even the trees and stones spoke to him with greetings of peace wherever he went.

He began to feel the need to be alone to worship. The Ka'aba was full of idols. His people had completely forgotten the One God, the Lord of Ibrahim ﷺ. They worshipped any and every thing. There were 365 idols in the Ka'aba, a different god for each day of the year. Muhammad ﷺ began to spend time in the rocky hills outside Mecca, in a cave that overlooks the valley. He could see the Ka'aba but not its idols. There, in the quiet, by himself, he fasted and worshipped the One God.

One night, in Muhammad's ﷺ fortieth year, the huge and glittering form of the Archangel Jibrail ﷺ appeared filling the horizon before the opening of the cave. He greeted Muhammad ﷺ with greetings of peace and then told him that Allah had created him to be His prophet. It is said that the Prophet ﷺ was so amazed that he would have fallen off the cliff had not Jibrail ﷺ caught him in his wings. Hugging him hard until his breath was almost gone, Jibrail ﷺ commanded, "Read." Muhammad ﷺ gasped that he could not, for in fact he had never learned to read. But Jibrail ﷺ was not ordering Muhammad ﷺ

to read from a book but rather to read and recite what the angel was pouring into his heart. Jibrail ﷺ recited some verses of the Qur'an, the last and final Book of Allah. Muhammad ﷺ repeated them, light upon light. Many, many times over the next 22 years Jibrail ﷺ delivered portions of this Qur'an to be recited to the people. Little by little it was revealed.

At first Muhammad ﷺ only told his family. Then he told close friends. They told others. Soon there was a group of believers who warmed themselves by the light of Muhammad's ﷺ face. People made fun of them but let them be.

Then everything changed. Allah commanded that His prophet Muhammad ﷺ make a general announcement and invite all of his family and tribe to believe in Allah, their Creator. The people who he thought loved and respected him, the people who had believed and trusted him in all their dealings up until then, turned away from him. They laughed and rejected his invitation with scorn. By Allah's permission Muhammad ﷺ ordered the full moon to split in half. Still they refused to believe and they began to hate him for bringing change and for being chosen above them.

Now things became difficult in Mecca for the Prophet ﷺ and the believers. The slaves and the poor without protection were tortured and even killed. All the Muslims were shunned. No one talked to them. No one bought from them or sold to them. No one had dealings with them of any kind. Muhammad's ﷺ beloved wife Khadija ﷺ died. But the Meccans were not ready to go so far as to kill Muhammad ﷺ because his uncle Abu Talib ﷺ still protected him. Then Abu Talib ﷺ died and Muhammad's ﷺ life was in danger.

At this, the lowest point in his life, without close family and protection, Allah took His Prophet ﷺ to Himself. Allah sent Jibrail ﷺ with the beautiful Buraq, a heavenly creature, covered in jewels, with the body of a horse and the head of a woman. The Prophet ﷺ mounted the gentle Buraq and flew to Jerusalem where all the earlier prophets had gathered, and he led them in prayer. They prayed behind him and gave him their greetings of peace. Then Muhammad ﷺ was given a tour of the seven Heavens, their wonders, their angels and their inhabitants. He saw also the seven Hells and their punishments. Then Allah honored him by drawing him close, closer than any creature had ever come before, even the angels. Within two bow lengths of Allah's Presence, the Prophet ﷺ approached. There he talked directly to Allah. He received the prayer and its five appointed times. When he came back he knew no more real sadness. He had completed the journey to Allah and he had returned.

Muhammad's ﷺ story is like so many of the other prophets. Rejected and threatened by his own people, he was forced to flee and seek shelter in another town. The small oasis of Yathrib offered Muhammad ﷺ sanctuary. All the believers left Mecca for Yathrib in 622 CE.

Muhammad's ﷺ story is similar to many of the others stories but his life is history. He is the only prophet who was sent in historical times when everything was written down and recorded. Qur'an was written as soon as it was revealed. So was every word and every action of the beloved Prophet who brought it. It is not just the outlines of his story that we know today. We know even the smallest details. We know the colors he liked and the food he preferred, how he sat and slept and ate, what he said and how he said it. It is not just his Book, the Qur'an, which he left for us as a guide; it is his whole life, every gesture, every smile, every move and word.

In appearance, they say, Muhammad ﷺ was neither tall nor short, neither fat nor thin. He was of average height and sturdy build. His hair was dark, neither lank nor curly, with some waviness in it. There was little or no gray in his beard. He was light skinned. His eyes were dark and luminous with long lashes. His teeth were straight and white. His face was slightly round. His smile lit up the world and his frown darkened it. When he looked, he really saw, and whoever really saw him, loved him

He was humble and patient. He never turned away from anyone. He had compassion for all, even a sickly kitten asleep on his cloak which he tore so as not to wake her when he moved. He was thankful for any gift, however small. In company he was gentle and smiling. In private he cried and begged Allah for forgiveness. He milked his own goats. He washed and mended his own clothes. He served his family. He never owned a bed but slept on palm branches on the ground. He wore cotton clothes and a turban of seven arm lengths. Green was his favorite color and he loved the smell of good perfume.

The Muslims were welcomed in Yathrib, which came to be called the Prophet's City, Madinat-an-Nabi, or just Madina. Men and women came from all over to learn from him and give him their support. His community included all kinds of people, men and women, young and old of all colors and backgrounds. There were Persians, Greeks, and Africans, as well as Arabs. There were those from wealthy families and those who had nothing but the clothes they were wearing. For the first time a Book had been sent, not to one

Muhammad ﷺ

"And We sent you as a mercy to all the worlds." (21:107)

small community, but to all the children of Nuh ﷺ; a Prophet and a Book for all the world. People, who before becoming Muslim would have never even spoken to each other, now lived together as brothers. One love united their hearts into one heart. That love was for the Prophet Muhammad ﷺ and the One God Who had made them all.

Muhammad ﷺ became their prophet and their ruler. When the tribes of Mecca made war on Madina, the Prophet ﷺ became a general. When the unbelievers lost the battles and asked for a treaty, Muhammad ﷺ became a statesman. When finally Allah gave the Muslims victory over the unbelievers, Muhammad ﷺ had the satisfaction of seeing each of the men who for twenty years had tortured and killed his followers, accept Islam and be forgiven. Husband, father, merchant, statesman, general, ruler, prophet, Muhammad ﷺ was them all.

When he died in Madina in 632 CE at age sixty-three, Muhammad ﷺ left the Qur'an and his example, the Sunnah, as a guide, not for just his family or the people of Arabia, but for all humankind. The Muslims spread throughout the world bringing Allah's religion and love for His Prophet ﷺ to every corner of the earth.

And although the journey of the light of prophethood ended with Muhammad ﷺ, the light is not gone. It still shines from his descendants and his friends, the saints, who will carry it as a lamp for us to find and to follow until the end of time.

May Allah bless Muhammad ﷺ and give him peace and help us to follow his light wherever we may find it. Amin.

www.ingramcontent.com/pod-product-compliance
Lightning Source LLC
LaVergne TN
LVHW060152080526
838202LV00052B/4142